BAY AREA
Backroads
BY DOUG McCONNELL

with Jerry Emory   Photographs by Stacy Geiken

CHRONICLE BOOKS
SAN FRANCISCO

Printed in China

All photographs in this book were made using Kodak film, processed by Vision Color Lab, and made using Nikon cameras and lenses.

Library of Congress Cataloging-in-Publication Data available.

ISBN 0-8118-2091-2

Front cover: top, East Brother Light Station, San Pablo Strait; center, Yosemite National Park; bottom, Doug McConnell
Back cover: Olmstead Point, Yosemite National Park
Page i: Abbotts Lagoon, Point Reyes National Seashore

Design: Rebecca S. Neimark, Twenty-Six Letters

Distributed in Canada by Raincoast Books, 8680 Cambie Street, Vancouver, B.C. V6P 6M9

10 9 8 7 6 5 4 3

Chronicle Books
85 Second Street
San Francisco, CA 94105

www.chroniclebooks.com

Acknowledgments

This book grows directly out of KRON-TV's *Bay Area Backroads* television series. Many people deserve credit for the success of the television program and the content of the book.

We must begin by saluting all the people who have watched *Bay Area Backroads* over the years. They have inspired us, told us what they like and what they don't, and given us many of our best story ideas. We hear from our viewers in many ways: by mail, by phone, through our Web site at www.sfgate.com, and by thousands of chance and informal encounters out in the community. We treasure this relationship–it's one of the great joys of doing this work, and it's matched by our affection for all the people we meet along the way and feature in our programs. Their passionately told stories are the lifeblood of *Bay Area Backroads*.

We owe a debt to Chronicle Publishing President and CEO John Sias, to Chronicle Broadcasting President and CEO Amy McCombs, to KRON Vice President and Station Manager Al Holzer, and to Janette Gitler, Director of KRON Local Programming and of BayTV. They set clear and high expectations but have given us the freedom and the time to travel our own path. Freedom and time are the two rarest commodities in broadcasting; without them, the television series would have foundered long ago. And this book would not have been published without the enthusiastic support of Chronicle Books President and Publisher Jack Jensen.

No one, day in and day out, deserves more credit for the success of the television series and the completion of this book than Executive Producer Carl Bidleman. His passion for the landscape and the people who enrich it has given *Backroads* its heart. His senses of humor and irony have kept us from taking ourselves too seriously. He has developed and managed a team of people who rarely miss a beat and who have learned much from his relentless attention to detail, his fine storytelling skills, and his straightforward decency and honesty.

The same qualities of humanity, wit, talent, and genuine enthusiasm for the task at hand are shared by every member of the *Backroads* crew, present and past. This book is theirs more than anyone's. They have poured themselves into every story. They have brought insight and creativity and a sense of fun to their efforts. Countless thanks and kudos go to producers Mary Stephens, Jeannette Regala, Stacy Waters, and Adrianna Roome; video photographers Jack Uhalde, Dick Williams, and Rick Greenwell; editors Libby Frankcom, Dave Vandergriff, Steve McConnell, Chuck Joyce, and Mike Morgan; book researchers Michelle Foronda and Drew Burns. A special note of thanks goes to story producers Michael Rosenthal and Dan Herz. Many of the words in this book were theirs first, often conceived late at night after hours of agonizing over the endless possibilities that every story holds.

We are also grateful to writer Jerry Emory, who did a superb job transforming our TV scripts into the chapters of this book, and to photographer Stacy Geiken, who retraced our steps in the teeth of an El Niño winter to capture the images that interpret these stories.

Our thanks to Chronicle Books Assistant Editor Joni Owen and Design Manager Pamela Geismar for their valuable assistance and unending patience in working with a crew so often unavailable while traveling the backroads.

Finally, we need to thank the spouses, significant others, and children of the *Backroads* crew for putting up with our long hours and many nights on the road. We hope it's been worth it to them. We doubt it always has been, but we couldn't have produced all of this without them. My wife, Kathy, is my best friend and best critic, and has set records for her patience and support. My children, Nicolas and Patrick, always remind me that no matter how much I love traveling the backroads, there's no place like home.

Contents

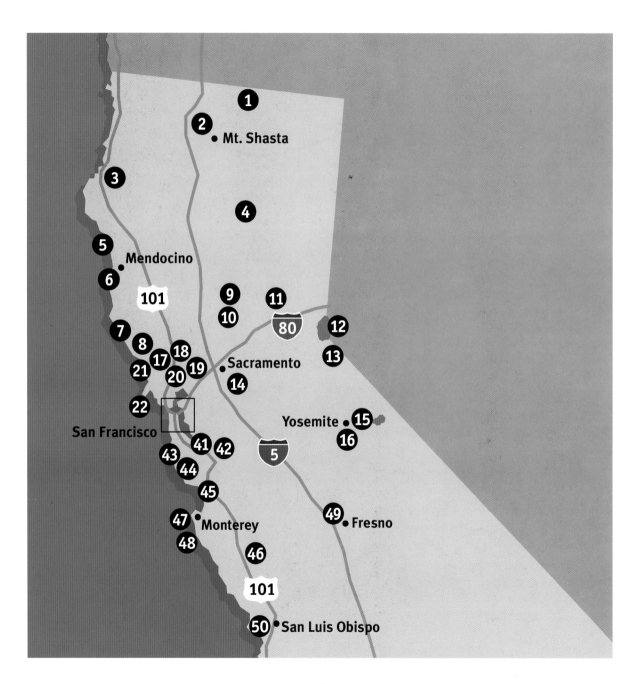

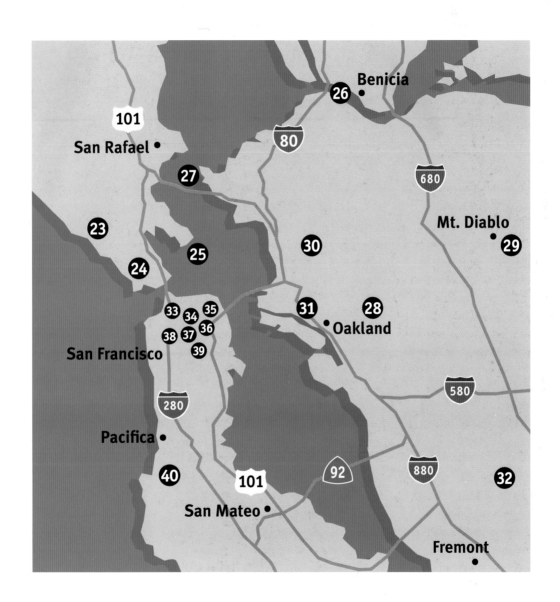

Introduction BY DOUG MCCONNELL

I'm writing this on a bright spring afternoon. I've driven to one of my favorite spots by the Bay to soak up the sun's warmth after a cool, wet winter and to seek a little inspiration. A slight breeze ripples the water. A few chatty gulls give their advice. The San Francisco skyline seems to float on the Bay just beyond the forested ridgelines of historic Angel Island. Altogether, not a bad office.

I have the good fortune to work in places like this nearly every day. It's my job to explore the Bay Area and Northern California, to get to know this beautiful region and its diverse people, and to pass along what I find to those who watch *Bay Area Backroads* on KRON and BayTV. Since 1985 the television program has reached hundreds of thousands of homes every week. I've had the privilege of hosting and serving as senior editor for the show since 1993. People tune in to learn about the little-known and very special people and places that populate the backroads of Northern California. And they also watch to help plan their own forays off the beaten track, which is what we hope you will do with this book.

The creation of the television series is a team effort. I work with a bright and talented group of producers, photographers, and editors who have taught me much and have also become my close friends over the years. This book is a product of our collaboration. We all report to a television station that has given us great freedom to learn, to grow, and to improve the quality of our storytelling. For me, all of this adds up to the best job in television. Not the biggest or most important job, but the best job.

I am doing what I would do if I didn't have to work for a living. And I am following backroads my mother and father encouraged me to appreciate long ago. My passion for travel and discovery and my love for Northern California came from them, and from my mother's father. He was born in the Contra Costa County town of Brentwood in 1883. As I grew up, he regaled me with stories about the way California used to be. He inspired my affection for the place, but he didn't have to work too hard to do that.

I always knew that Northern California was special. After all, the rugged coast, the high Sierra, the culturally fascinating cities, and the wildlands of the seaside hills, the Delta, and the Central Valley are all in our backyard. But I didn't fully realize how special this region is until I went away for quite awhile.

For almost twenty years I lived far afield, from the East Coast to Alaska. I came back to the Bay Area in 1983, and began to rediscover my home. I followed the backroads of my childhood, seeing the area with fresh eyes and falling in love with it all over again, this time head-over-heels and far more deeply than ever before. I had seen wonders all over the world, but I had found no place more blessed than this. And best of all, despite all the changes that occurred during my years away, much of what my parents and grandfather had known and shown me was still around.

I found that the past had not been entirely paved. The land had not been completely engulfed by urban sprawl. All the roads were not interstate freeways. All the hotels and restaurants were not simply links in vast chains. All the wild animals were not confined to zoos, books, and fond memories. California was struggling with rapid growth, but its heart still beat strongly. Many of California's towns looked like Anywhere, USA, but the state's cultural personality is still colorful and complex.

There were reasons for me to grieve for what had vanished while I was gone: ranches, farms, and open space in and around our expanding cities; crowdless summer days in Yosemite Valley; and clean air year-round in the Sacramento Valley. But there were also reasons to celebrate what had been gained in my absence: the return of elephant seals to the coast; the creation of the finest urban park in the world, the Golden Gate National Recreation Area; and the increased openness in many communities to people of all races and cultures. I found that California was certainly imperfect, but that the better angels of its soul still flourished, and that I could encounter them along the backroads.

The backroads are two-lane blacktops, dirt tracks, mountain trails, rivers, bays, and city streets. They are the paths less traveled. They require some time and patience and a genuine desire to be surprised. They are the right roads for people who don't know what to expect around the next bend, but want to find out. The rules of these roads are few but important: be prepared to slow down, pull over, and visit for a while, and remember that getting there is as good as being there.

These backroads have led my colleagues and me into big cities, tiny towns, and wide-open spaces, to meet people with stories to tell, lessons to teach, and time to give. The backroads have led us to environments we'll never forget, relationships that'll last a lifetime, hilarious moments we relive every day, and ideas that have changed the way we think and have influenced what we believe. Our backroads adventures have given us hope that all the world is not falling apart, and

that many people are doing a good job of passing it along to our children. Our adventures have also given us plenty of tales to tell, which brings us to the content of this book.

What follows are fifty of our favorite journeys and destinations in the Bay Area and Northern California. They are all accessible to explorers of the backroads. With the help of writer Jerry Emory and

Before traveling the backroads, it's a good idea to call ahead to find out about special events, weather conditions, etc. We've included telephone numbers and a few Web site addresses of the places we visit in this book. *Bay Area Backroads* also maintains a Web site with travel tips and many of our past stories. Our Web site can be accessed directly or via The Gate, the Web site of the Chronicle Publishing Company.

Bay Area Backroads
www.bayareabackroads.com
The Gate www.sfgate.com

photographer Stacy Geiken, we describe some of our most memorable experiences, and pass along tips about what to see and do and how to travel. The exceptional photographs that brighten these pages don't just illustrate what we've seen, but capture some of what we've felt. Through these pictures and words, we hope that you'll have a sense of being along with us for the ride, and that you'll be encouraged to head out on your own.

When you do head out, we have one last piece of advice and a request. First, the advice: In this turn-of-the-millennium world rushing hell-bent toward homogenization, look for those distinctive and unusual people out there who are passionate about where they live and who choose to lead lives of their own creation. They've made interesting choices that they've had to think about and stand by. They always have something to say, typically seasoned with a keen sense of humor. They are the true stars of *Bay Area Backroads*, on television and in these pages.

And finally, our request: Send us your tales of travel. You'll have something to say too that we should hear, and backroads to suggest that we should follow. And if you see us along the way, please follow the rules of the road: Slow down, pull over, and visit for awhile.

The North Coast and the Cascades

From left: Boiling Springs Lake (Tour 4) and Main Street, Mendocino (Tour 6)

THE KLAMATH BASIN:
Big, Wide, Wonderful, and Waterfowl

Many people are fascinated by the beauty and the power of Mount Shasta, the fourteen-thousand-foot dormant volcano that dominates northern California's landscape. For many people—past and present—it's a profoundly spiritual place and the gateway to an untrammeled and magical region.

Just northeast of Mount Shasta, straddling the California-Oregon border, is the Klamath Basin, a territory rich in natural beauty and human legends. In the wintertime, it's home to the highest density of waterfowl in all California and the largest concentration of bald eagles in the lower forty-eight states. A good portion of the basin has been designated as the Lower Klamath National Wildlife Refuge.

Bay Area naturalist Michael Ellis—a frequent guide for the *Backroads* crew—leads trips throughout California and the world. Every year he brings a group of adventurous souls to the basin in winter. "The Klamath Basin has big open skies and broad expanses," says Michael, surveying the landscape. "You can see for miles and miles, and in many ways it's unlike the rest of California."

It's about a seven-hour trip from San Francisco, up Interstate 5 past Redding to Weed, then northeast on Highway 97. Once here you can explore an expanse of a thousand square miles, from Lava Beds National Monument to Klamath Falls in Oregon. Not too many people know about this area, which is part of the attraction.

The signs of civilization are few and far between up here. The occasional little towns you do encounter, such as Dorris, are struggling to be noticed. To attract visitors, Dorris residents are raising money to build the world's tallest flagpole, and they're almost there. They say the flagpole will rise about two hundred feet off the ground—not quite as tall as Mount Shasta!

Mount Shasta looms over the horizon, giving the whole area a larger-than-life feel. Local Native American tribes consider the mountain very sacred; it's also revered by some new-age spiritualists. Even when it's obscured by clouds, Shasta's influence is not diminished. The clouds seem bigger here, the wind more powerful, and the rainbows more brilliant.

Perhaps that's why the Bear Valley National Wildlife Refuge—about one mile west of Worden, Oregon, off Highway 97—is one of the prime roosting spots for

Mount Shasta from the Klamath Basin

Lower Klamath National Wildlife Refuge

bald eagles. The roosting areas are off-limits to humans, but it's easy to get a good view from nearby as the eagles fly out each morning to forage and hunt. Make sure you get there just before sunrise, though.

A few decades ago, bald eagles were on the verge of extinction in California

and elsewhere, largely because of heavy use of the pesticide DDT. With the help of the Endangered Species Act, the birds have made a remarkable recovery. In addition to eagles, you'll have plenty of opportunities to see red-tailed hawks, rough-legged hawks, ravens, and marsh hawks throughout the basin. The basin

is also a favorite habitat for tundra swans.

On the southern edge of the basin's verdant and beautiful expanse is Lava Beds National Monument, the site of a very ugly chapter in American history. In 1872 and 1873 on these lava-covered lands, the Modoc Indian War was waged

Lower Klamath National Wildlife Refuge

Pat McMillan is director of the Klamath County Museum in Klamath Falls, Oregon, about thirty-five miles north of the lava beds. It's a good place to learn about both the natural and the human history of the area. "At the time," says Pat, "if the Modocs had been given a reservation—even a large reservation where they wanted it—it would have been a very reasonable cost to the United States government. The war cost several million dollars, and it would have cost probably sixty thousand dollars for a reservation—and a much less tragic story."

Today there's a nature path through Captain Jack's stronghold in the Lava Beds National Monument, so it's a little easier to get around and delve into the volcanic origins of the Mount Shasta region. From amazing waterfowl and congregating eagles to fascinating hikes through a once-tragic landscape, the Klamath Basin offers countless unexpected adventures.

against a desperate group of Native Americans. Actually, it was a contest between more than three hundred U.S. cavalry and volunteers and a less organized group of some fifty Modoc Indians, including women and children. The Modocs were being forced from their ancestral home to make way for settlers. They refused to leave the area, instead fleeing into a dark and tumbled landscape of sharp lava, often cloaked in dense fog coming from

nearby lakes. Out-manned and out-gunned, they employed their shrewdness and knowledge of the strange terrain to hold off the cavalry for five months.

The Modoc warriors—intriguing characters with anglicized names such as Curly-Haired Jack, Scarface Charley, and their leader, Captain Jack—inflicted heavy casualties on the U.S. soldiers before they were finally captured. Four Modocs were executed; the rest were banished to a reservation in Oklahoma.

Klamath Basin National Wildlife Complex (including Bear Valley) 530-667-2231
Klamath County Museum, Oregon
541-883-4208
Lava Beds National Monument
530-667-2282
Michael Ellis's Footloose Forays
707-829-1844

CALIFORNIA'S MYSTICAL NORTHERN LANDSCAPE

The *Backroads* crew always enjoys returning to the scenic and historic neighborhood of Mount Shasta, the largest volcano in the continental United States.

Shasta is a mountain of many moods. The towering slopes stir the human imagination. Some people say that it's a landing pad for spacecraft. Aliens or not, there is no arguing that Shasta soars skyward while presiding over a wild region filled with both natural and human history, and a strong railroading culture.

About a five-hour drive north from San Francisco on Interstate 5 will get you here. This northern realm of the Golden State has been home to *San Francisco Examiner* outdoor columnist Tom Stienstra for many years. Although Tom has the advantage of seeing the region from the windows of his own plane, most of us will be more than content exploring its backroads on the ground.

"There's no place on earth like Mount Shasta," says Tom. "You can draw a fifty-mile circle around it, look around, and soon realize it's the most beautiful place in the world. When I fly out of Dunsmuir it is phenomenal to me what I can see in just a few minutes. To the north is the Shasta-Trinity National Forest. There is

also the Mount Eddie Range, Scott Mountain, the Trinity Alps, and the jagged spires of Castle Crags State Park—a fantastic place for camping and hiking."

Other highlights are Shasta Lake, the McCloud River, and the humble beginnings of a great river, the Sacramento. "Did you know that the Sacramento River bubbles up from the earth in a public park in Mount Shasta City?" says Tom. "And from here it runs some four hundred river miles to San Francisco Bay, through everything that makes California great—the mountains, the Central Valley, and San Francisco Bay."

California's mightiest river, Castle Crags' granite steeples, and Mount Shasta itself are all part of a remarkable region known to many in these parts as the State of Jefferson. "They wanted to make this entire region—from Castle Crags to Ashland, Oregon—the State of Jefferson back in the 1940s," laughs Tom. Jefferson never became our fifty-first state, but for many it is still a state of mind.

Your exploration of the Shasta region proceeds as you head into the little town of Dunsmuir. Nestled in a forested canyon at the southern edge of Mount Shasta alongside Interstate 5, Dunsmuir has the

Yreka Western Railroad

feel of an old, hard-working town with a long railroading history.

Trains have been rolling through Dunsmuir since 1886. In fact, 10 percent of the town's 2,300 people still work for the railroad. There's even an official guide available in town to photographing trains in the scenic terrain near Dunsmuir. It's such a railroading mecca that some aficionados, such as Bruce Petty, have made their homes here.

"If you're going to live in Dunsmuir," says Bruce with a laugh, "you've got to have a train, and you've got to have a

train set. That's all there is to it." Bruce moved here from southern California in 1975 to immerse himself in the life of the rails. Today he works in a little shop overlooking the tracks where he collects and restores railroad parts.

According to Bruce, Dunsmuir may be the best locale for train spotting, but it's not the only railroading town in the State of Jefferson. From Dunsmuir's wooded canyons, head north on Interstate 5 past Mount Shasta, into a broad valley with sweeping vistas. In forty-five minutes the town of Yreka appears, and the

region's railroading tradition continues.

"I'm commonly known as the railroad maggot of Yreka," jokes Larry Bacon, the General Manager of the Yreka Western Railroad—a railway in continuous operation since 1889. Since 1987, a local club has maintained a 1,500-square-foot replica of the Yreka Western Railroad—and the places it passes through—in a converted train depot. But most folks venture to Yreka to ride Larry's Bluegoose Steamtrain, which he calls the "Bullet Train" of Yreka. He says the Bluegoose actually reaches speeds approaching ten miles per hour, gradually pulling passengers through this region's rolling ranchlands from May through October. It's a casual, colorful, and quite wonderful journey back in time.

Interestingly, Yreka was once named the capital of the State of Jefferson and a "governor" was actually sworn in. Judge Eddie Reagan became Governor in a tongue-in-cheek ceremony on December 4, 1941. His reign was eclipsed three days later when Pearl Harbor was bombed, but playful fantasies of statehood linger on in this landscape of volcanoes, forests, parklands, and railroads.

Dunsmuir Visitor Center 800-Dunsmuir
Yreka Western Railroad and the
Bluegoose Steamtrain 800-Yrekarr

Left: Mount Shasta; above: Larry Bacon at the Yreka Western Railroad

SEEKING BIGFOOT:
From Avenue of the Giants to the Klamath River

From its ancient and massive redwoods, to its rough and secluded coastline, to its rambunctious rivers and remote canyons, northwestern California is big enough and wild enough to contain a legend.

Some people up here claim they've

Avenue of the Giants

seen a creature they call Bigfoot, with hair like a bear but the body of a man. Others are skeptical. But the fact remains that nobody in these woods can prove that Bigfoot exists—and they can't entirely disprove it either. Real or not, the creature has been good for the tourist trade in these parts, and it's captured the imagination of visitors and residents alike.

Whether you are a Bigfoot believer or not, this part of the world is a great place to explore. In an area such as this, where there's still room for a legend to wander, you never know what you'll find along the backroads.

Start your Bigfoot odyssey some two hundred miles north of San Francisco on Highway 101, beyond the towns of Myers Flat and Weott, where the Eel River divides. From there, follow various backroads and highways west and northward through the intriguing hamlets of Honeydew, Ferndale, Arcata, and Trinidad on the coast. Then, turn eastward into the deepest recesses of Bigfoot country—Willow Creek and the whitewater of the Klamath River.

You may not find Bigfoot at the very beginning of your journey, but you will find lots of big trees. The Avenue of the Giants is a detour right through ancient redwood groves. It's an unusual combination of natural wonders and human curiosities—such as drive-through redwoods and bizarre treehouses.

From the Avenue of the Giants near the fork of the Eel River, turn onto a route that wanders through the coastal range, the Mattole Road. You'll climb steeply out of the redwoods and onto high ridgelines with dramatic vistas. Soon you'll move back downslope and descend into an isolated river valley and tiny Honeydew, one of California's smallest towns. At last count the population was skyrocketing— it's about seven people! The road often washes out during heavy winter storms, which can dump up to one hundred and sixty inches of rain a year here.

Bob Shinn is Honeydew's town father in more ways than one. One of Honeydew's newest residents is his son, Wes. The entire metropolis of Honeydew consists of Bob's combination gas station, post office, and general store. He even carries some videos, for those locals with electricity. Bob's General Store is the place to stock up on necessities for the backroads. If you ask Bob about Bigfoot, he will most likely point you north, toward serious Bigfoot country.

Next stop: Ferndale (downright large with some 1,400 residents). Follow the coast on one of the most scenic drives in California, Mattole Road. Along the way it careens up and down steep mountains and skirts a few lonely and lovely beaches perfect for a Bigfoot or two.

Ferndale is like a living museum, a

Victorian heirloom. In fact, the entire community has been declared a state historical landmark. Ferndale is also known as the town built on butterfat, and dairy farming still plays a big role here. Just go over to the fairgrounds, and you'll see the prominently displayed headstones of three legendary and highly productive cows. "We have our heroes," laughs Hobart Brown, a sculptor, philosopher, and self-appointed Ferndale promoter, "and our heroes happen to be cows!" Cows and loggers are now sharing center stage with Ferndale's many artists; Hobart opened the town's first art gallery back in the early sixties.

If you want to spend a little time here, Ferndale has some nice motels and bed-and-breakfast inns. The community has remade itself many times, after floods, earthquakes, and economic declines—all the while keeping a tight hold on its history.

Ferndale's eclectic nature makes it open to all sorts of possibilities, so when folks drop by looking for Bigfoot, no one even bats an eye. Still, Bigfoot rumors will probably propel you farther north, toward Humboldt Bay.

Consider venturing to Arcata on the northern lip of Humboldt Bay, some twenty-nine miles from Ferndale on Highway 101. Arcata is also home to Humboldt State University and the Arcata Marsh

Bob and Weston Shinn at Bob's General Store

and Wildlife Sanctuary, a manufactured wilderness helping to keep the town and Humboldt Bay clean.

The marsh, on the south side of Arcata, was once a county dump. Says Arcata resource specialist Julie Neander, "It's very different now because of the commitment a lot of people in Arcata decided to make in the 1970s." Arcata changed yesteryear's dump into today's sewage treatment facility. The vegetation planted here helps clean Arcata's wastewater while providing a new oasis for wildlife—and people, who come down just to walk or jog or have a picnic. Many visit to learn about the habitats and

habits of the many species of birds that flourish here. People even climb the old dump called Mount Trashmore—now covered with native plants. The birdwatching from this vantage point is spectacular, but sad to say, not a single Bigfoot has ever been spotted.

From Arcata drive a few miles north to the picturesque village of Trinidad, suspended precariously above the sea. Trinidad is popular with folks seeking to escape the pressures of city life. Town resident Patti Fleschner came here for a visit and never left. "Trinidad was going to be a harbor as big as San Francisco one day, but San Francisco somehow became more popular. Today, I think people come here for the quiet, to relax, and to be away from phones, faxes, and the things that get to people in the larger cities."

Trinidad is here because the ocean is. Fishing sustained the town for generations, and those who braved the turbulent sea are not forgotten. The Memorial Lighthouse of Trinidad was built to remember the local fishermen who died at sea. The sea isn't tame here, and neither is its relationship to the land. They seem to tear at each other with dramatic results that startle the eye.

Immediately north of town is Patrick's Point State Park. It's not a gentle place—the land's end feels like the edge of the earth—but somehow the park's effect on people is calming. A dense forest shrouds the landscape in a moist, dark-green blanket. The forest finds its way to a place where the land suddenly falls away to the churning sea many feet below. The breathtaking scenery makes it a perfect spot for weddings.

As far as we know, Bigfoot never exchanged vows here, but perhaps he has about an hour and a half to the east. Highway 299 leads east to Willow Creek, known as the gateway to Bigfoot country. A large statue of Bigfoot is right downtown. Resident Darlene Mesunas says she saw Bigfoot in the woods nearby when

The Gingerbread Mansion, Ferndale

she was ten or eleven years old. "I saw this huge thing. It didn't make any noise. It didn't growl. But that whole area smelled like a garbage dump. The smell was terrible. It was like something rotten."

Darlene hesitates to tell her story for fear that people will think she's just got a big imagination, even though this landscape has spawned tales of a big and elusive creature since Native Americans arrived thousands of years ago. But hard evidence is in short supply.

Willow Creek resident Al Hodgsen took a casting of what is allegedly a Bigfoot footprint. "The tracks were there. I didn't fake them, but I can't prove that somebody else didn't fake them. I've never heard a Bigfoot, but they tell me they make a particular sound and if you hear it once, you never forget it."

Al grew up here, and he tends to believe in Bigfoot. He says he's not surprised the creature has had little direct contact with people. "For example," he explains, "there are so many bears living around here it's unreal, but you rarely see a bear. The same's probably true with Bigfoot."

Although Bigfoot overcrowding is clearly no problem around Willow Creek, turn north to continue your quest to see or smell one along the Klamath River on Highway 96. Most sightings have been reported along the Klamath, sometimes reluctantly.

"I don't even talk to anybody about it anymore," says Rusty Briscoe. "Everybody gives me such a bad time about it, so I just leave it alone." Rusty says that late one recent night, he and his brother Josh drove right by Bigfoot. "At first I thought it was a bear. But it had long, shaggy hair, and it was tan, and it was standing on two legs! As soon as our car lights came up and hit him, he just turned, took one jump, and he was on top of a ridge and gone through the brush." So if Bigfoot exists, he's a great athlete as well as being tan, tall, tail-less, and smelly, and he knows his way around these woods in the dark.

Shirley Reynolds lives in the village of Orleans, an area that's so remote anything seems possible. "I run the Chamber Information Center," Shirley says, "and different people stop by. Some believe, and some just think it's a nice story. But they're still here looking!"

If you don't find Bigfoot while you're driving along the highway or backroad, why not try while rafting down the Klamath River? River guide Mike Charlton is a Bigfoot booster. "I believe that Bigfoot does exist," says the seasoned river rat, "and I believe that if he's to be found anywhere, this would be the place to find him."

But whether you're searching for Bigfoot or not, the Klamath is a river worth rafting. It's also a good way to see the wild terrain of northern California in the company of other spirited adventurers. The Klamath glides through a rugged landscape, populated by few people, many critters, and perhaps some Bigfeet.

It's comforting to know that there's still room in crowded California for the imagination to roam and leave unsolved a little mystery of nature.

Ferndale Chamber of Commerce
   707-786-4477
Arcata Chamber of Commerce
   707-822-3619
Trinidad Chamber of Commerce
   707-441-9827
Patrick's Point State Park 707-677-3570
Willow Creek Chamber of Commerce
   530-629-2693

Wedding Rock, Patrick's Point State Park

4 NORTHEASTERN ADVENTURES:
Lassen Peak, Ishi Country, and World Class Fishing

Although it's right in our own backyard, many of us have never visited Lassen Volcanic National Park. And that's too bad because it's one of the loveliest places in all of California. At Lassen, nature—in a very dramatic fashion—is still under construction.

The park is a land of boiling lakes and steaming earth. It's a region of pine-covered, snow-capped mountains and transparent streams filled with elusive trout. While it's peaceful here, you can see geologic history being made right before your eyes, and you can walk across places where violent eruptions once shook the earth. The 106,000 acres of this national park are accessible by car, by horseback, or by foot.

Lassen is about a five-hour drive northeast from the Bay Area. Take Interstate 5 to either Red Bluff or Redding and head east about fifty miles. Lassen is not much farther from the Bay Area than Yosemite, yet it averages only about four hundred thousand visitors annually compared to Yosemite's four million! Hiking up Lassen Peak is a popular excursion, and although most of the park sees relatively few people, this is one place where you might encounter a crowd in the summer.

The road through Lassen is beautiful. It twists and turns over the mountains, and you can see much of the park right from your car. There are marker signs along the way that interpret what you're seeing, so slow down, get out and explore a little bit, and you'll have a great time.

Manzanita Lake is just inside the northwest entrance to the park. It's worth the trip just to come here and fish, paddle a canoe, or enjoy the scenery. But Manzanita Lake is only a small part of what Lassen has to offer. There are more than fifty other lakes, seven hundred flowering plant species, and one hundred and fifty miles of hiking trails.

Lassen Peak, an impressive 10,457 feet, is the last volcano to have erupted in California. It rumbled sporadically from 1914 until 1921, but by far the most dramatic activity was in 1915, when a massive eruption sent a mushroom cloud seven miles into the sky. A year later the area was declared a national park. Today, you can see the world that eruption helped create.

Lassen Peak

Helen Lake, Lassen Volcanic National Park

According to park naturalist Scott Isaacson, this area has experienced volcanic activity for millions of years. "A lot of it is very recent, though, and that's what makes the park really exciting," he says.

There are four different types of volcanoes on earth, and all are in Lassen Park. Lassen Peak is one of the world's largest "plug dome" volcanoes—a very dangerous volcanic type. "They tend to erupt in a very violent fashion," explains Scott.

"You can still see clear evidence of that violence in the landscape and in the individual rocks."

As you ascend the mountain on the well-worn trail the landscape becomes more forbidding and stark. And yet among

Black Rock, Ishi Wilderness

raced down the mountain for miles.

Ideally, you should spend a few days in Lassen Park to do it justice. Accommodation options are rather limited, but there are ample campgrounds in the park and a few motels in the surrounding area. The only lodge located inside the park—the Drakesbad Guest Ranch—is also the hardest place to get into, but it's worth the effort. It's been welcoming visitors during summer months for more than a hundred years with rustic bungalows, terrific food, and a pool fed by natural hot springs. Many families have been coming here for generations.

From the stables at Drakesbad you can rent a horse (whether you're a guest or camping nearby) and ride with a wrangler, like Kacey Koeberer, to one of the park's most unusual features: Boiling Springs Lake. The water temperature in the lake is a toasty 125 degrees. You can smell the sulfur-laced waters before seeing them. Ringing the shore are several steaming mudpots—something else to look at, but not to touch.

Lassen presents an amazing contrast: the turbulent rumblings underground giving rise to a region of incredible beauty and tranquillity. "I love it," says Kacey. "I lived in the city for a long time and I love being up here. I love being out where you can see the stars at night and the moon." Lassen is a remarkable area where you

the pumice and stones you will find white bark pines clinging to the hillsides, as if hanging on for dear life. "These trees are survivors," says Scott. "This is a very harsh environment to eke out an existence when you consider they're covered with snow a large part of the year, then they're baking in the alpine sun all summer."

If you want to scale Lassen, make sure you bring plenty of water and food, take your time, and bring extra clothes because the weather can be a lot colder

up at the top. In fact, there's usually snow in the higher elevations year-round.

Standing at the top is breathtaking (remember you're almost at eleven thousand feet!). You can see Mount Shasta gleaming in the distance, as if it is floating on air. Northward you can view the "chaos crags," the park's youngest volcanoes. You can also look down on the remains of the 1915 eruption. When the lava flowed out of the mountaintop it mixed with snow and huge boulders weighing four to ten tons each. This deadly slurry then

can feel the earth breathe and witness its awesome power.

But Lassen Park is just part of the picture. If you follow the waters that flow south and west from Lassen Peak, you'll find yourself leaving the park and exploring a rugged landscape that played an important role in California's history: the Ishi Wilderness.

The forty-thousand-acre wilderness area is part of the Lassen National Forest. Getting here isn't easy. To reach the trails and creeks of the Ishi Wilderness, you bid farewell to well-paved highways and follow a winding dirt road that's virtually impassable during rainy weather. You can find popular trailheads out of Chico on Highway 32, or off of Highway 36 at Paynes Creek. It gets very hot in July and August, but in the spring and fall, it's definitely worth the journey. Because the Ishi Wilderness is so hard to reach, you're likely to have the place practically to yourself.

This area is named after Ishi, a Yahi Indian who lived alone in this rough terrain early in the twentieth century. The place has barely changed since then; you get the feeling he could still be out there in the volcanic landscape. Ishi was born in 1860, a time when white settlers were massacring his people. As the Indians' numbers plummeted, Ishi and his fellow survivors sought refuge here in this rough but beautiful land.

By 1908, Ishi was the only Yahi left. In 1911, he emerged from his remote sanctuary and entered the modern world. He carried with him a message of survival and simplicity and an intense understanding of and reverence for the natural world. This wilderness area not only stands as a living monument to Ishi, but also as part of our state's hope for the future. As development slowly creeps up to the edges of thus protected stronghold, we will continue to learn lessons from Ishi and the land he loved.

Nearly a hundred miles north of the Ishi Wilderness, on the other side of

---

DRAKESBAD AND ISHI

To call Drakesbad during the summer months, contact your long-distance operator and ask to be connected with the Susanville operator in area code 530. Then ask for Drakesbad Toll Station Number 2 and wait for an answer.

For people interested in the life of Ishi, you can find his artifacts right here in the Bay Area at the Phoebe A. Hearst Museum of Anthropology at U.C. Berkeley.

Lassen Peak, is a different type of natural site: Hat Creek and the Pit River. They are both more accessible than the Ishi Wilderness, and the lessons they teach tend to be about angling—fly-fishing in particular.

Hat Creek is a slow, clear stream where you can actually see the fish moving through the waters. The Pit River slides through a fabulous canyon about twenty-five miles long. Fishing guide Dick Galland knows these world-class waters like the back of his hand, and he loves to teach people how to fly fish in both. "There is a very Zen quality to fly-fishing," says Dick in a serious tone. "It is impossible, in my experience, to fly-fish and think about anything else at the same time."

From boiling lakes to mountaintop vistas, from magnificent wilderness areas to unequaled fishing streams, Lassen Volcanic National Park and its environs are a must-see for travelers of the backroads.

Lassen Volcanic National Park
530-595-4444
Drakesbad Guest Ranch
530-529-1512 or 530-529-9820
Ishi Wilderness 530-258-2141
**Phoebe A. Hearst Museum of
Anthropology** 510-643-7648
Dick Galland's Clearwater Trout Tours
415-381-1173

SINKYONE WILDERNESS:
Finding Yourself on the Lost Coast

The north coast of California can be a mysterious and somewhat intimidating landscape. It's often cloaked in varied shades of gray and green. But with time, you'll realize it's a soothing, almost nurturing place to be. In fact, it's the kind of place that grows on you very quickly.

In the wild and remote part of coastal northern Mendocino County—where it's possible to be the only human being for miles and miles—the land is commonly referred to as the Lost Coast, but it hasn't been lost for long.

Today the Lost Coast is easy to reach, but only if you're a bird. Roads are scarce and not always paved. The terrain is so imposing that Highway One turns inland to avoid it. To really understand this lost corner of California, seek out Sinkyone

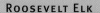

ROOSEVELT ELK

Several subspecies of elk inhabited North America when Europeans first arrived on this continent. Of the surviving groups, the Roosevelt elk, named for President Theodore Roosevelt, live in pockets throughout Pacific forests from northern California to British Columbia. Male elk can grow to one thousand pounds, eating a diet of mainly grasses. After moose, the Roosevelt elk is the largest member of North America's deer family.

The Lost Coast

Wilderness State Park on the southern portion of the Lost Coast. Drive north of San Francisco on Highway 101 about four hours to the community of Garberville, then head west about an hour on Briceland Road.

Even the easiest route into the Sinkyone Wilderness eventually turns to dirt, and sometimes it's impassable during winter rains. But those able to venture in are rewarded in grand style. As soon as you enter the park and the wilderness area, the first creatures you are likely to come across are Roosevelt elk, which some Native Americans called the wapiti.

Roosevelt elk were nearly wiped out in the 1800s by market hunters, but today they are thriving. The Sinkyone herd started when these majestic animals were reintroduced to the area in 1982.

Park Ranger Bill Wisehart is an expert on the Sinkyone. "Sometimes it's kind of a somber place," says Bill, referring to the fog that often blankets the coast in the summer and the storms that slam into it during the winter. "But other times," he continues, "you get this magnificent blue Pacific right in front of you and the area looks like Hawaii!"

A little farther along the road into the park you can see jumbled rocks rising out of the sunlit Pacific mist and waves crashing through twin arches. Where the road ends, the Lost Coast hiking trail picks up. It leads to ever more remote destinations that can take you an hour to reach, or three days.

An impressive grove of century-old non-native eucalyptus trees is only the first clue that part of this shoreline was once a hub of human activity. "You can see sections of the old railroad track in Bear Harbor," observes Bill. "The tracks led to a wharf from which lumber and other materials were shipped to a booming San Francisco." Today two lonely pieces of track protrude from a cliff above the harbor, listlessly pointing toward what used to be.

"A lot of these little places along the north coast, like Bear Harbor," Bill explains, "were at one time the more populated parts of California, and they were definitely not lost!" This coast was never really lost, just overlooked.

"The Native Americans who once lived here—the Sinkyones—said this was a healing place, and at times I feel that," says Bill. "You know, you can come here and you just feel better for having been here." It's a sometimes forgotten coast that you and nature have the pleasure of rediscovering.

Sinkyone Wilderness State Park
707-986-7711

Roosevelt elk

6 MENDOCINO: California's New England

Living so close to many wonderful places, Bay Area residents can easily turn a couple of days into a vacation. Within a few hours, most of us can get away to Big Sur, Napa Valley, Yosemite National Park, or the Bay Area's own New England, the village of Mendocino.

Mendocino, which has been called "Cape Cod shipped around the Horn," is about 150 miles north of San Francisco. Several routes will get you here, but the most direct takes you up Highway 101 to Cloverdale, then out to the coast via Route 128.

Mendocino looks out of place and out of time. Perched on a bluff above the sea, it has the feel of a small hamlet on the New England coast about a hundred years ago. Some streets are lined with saltbox houses, others with Victorian mansions surrounded by picket fences.

Mendocino grew up in the 1850s around a lumber mill that processed wood from the area's redwood forests. Today it's a good spot to get away from the daily grind of modern life.

To get a good look at Mendocino, and to help you ease into a nineteenth-century frame of mind, you can take a carriage ride through town guided by a local resident, such as Kelly Daoust. "You know, one hundred years ago this was a tough little town," says Kelly. "It was a logging

Mendocino

town. I think there were about seven bordellos here during that time. So it was pretty wild."

These days Mendocino thrives on tourism. "It takes two days to cover the entire town if you go into every shop," says Kelly. "And every shop is worth going into! It's really unique stuff, and a lot of it's locally made."

Since the 1950s, Mendocino has been a haven for artists. You'll find galleries on virtually every street. And the Mendocino Art Center welcomes visitors to watch artists at work. The visitors center on Main Street is also worth a stop.

As charming as the village is, perhaps Mendocino's best attraction is its rugged coastline and quiet little coves. Mendocino Headlands State Park, one of a dozen or so nearby state parks, is just across the street from town. You can walk out of the shops and into nature's kingdom, and there's plenty of room to get away from the crowds during peak times of the year.

November through March is prime whale-watching time, and this is prime whale-watching territory. Look for paths that lead you along the ocean's edge and down to several beaches where you can gaze out and perhaps spot migrating gray whales. Dogs on leashes are welcome, too.

A stone's throw north of Mendocino is Russian Gulch State Park, a popular place for camping. Hikers will find miles of

Noyo Harbor

trails, including one that leads to the thirty-foot-high Russian Gulch Falls.

At MacKerricher State Park, just a couple of miles north near Fort Bragg, you can ride a bicycle along the coast, stop and explore some wonderful beaches, have a picnic, or just watch the sunset. A paved logging road within the park is closed to vehicle traffic, but is great for biking, walking, and for those using wheelchairs.

If you love flowers, the Mendocino Botanical Gardens are forty acres of heaven, with a variety of gardens blooming each season. Another favorite attraction, especially for families, is the Skunk

Train, which leaves the coast in Fort Bragg for a ride through the redwood forests.

Mendocino is such a wonderful getaway that sometimes it gets pretty crowded. So if you need to get away from the getaway, Noyo Harbor is a good place to do it. It's in Fort Bragg, and it's a real working fishing port. The sights and the smells of the sea are terrific.

If you ask Kelly when to visit Mendocino, she will say June is a gorgeous month. October is also beautiful, not as colorful as spring, but warm and often clear of fog, and there aren't as many people because school is back in session.

In many ways, Mendocino is the perfect short getaway from the Bay Area. It's so close, and yet it seems so far away—a slice of New England and old California along the backroads.

Mendocino Coast Chamber of Commerce
707-961-6300
Mendocino Coast State Parks
707-937-5804
Mendocino Botanical Gardens
707-937-3069
Skunk Train 800-777-5865

Fort Ross State Historic Park

JENNER TO POINT ARENA:
Cruising the Colorful Coast of Sonoma and Mendocino Counties

The coastal countryside of Sonoma and Mendocino Counties is magical and unpredictable. With ever-changing terrain, weather, and lighting conditions, its mood can shift dramatically from one moment to the next. The only constant is its beauty.

Begin your trip about two hours north of San Francisco in the Sonoma County town of Jenner, alongside the mouth of the Russian River. Then head north on Highway One, certainly one of the most scenic coastal road trips anywhere in the world. You'll pass Fort Ross and Salt Point State Park en route to Point Arena in Mendocino County.

Jenner is a very pleasant wide spot in the road with a few places to eat and stay. It also has a commanding view of the Russian River's plunge into the Pacific. Harbor seals often sun themselves on the beach below, keeping a wary eye out for the great white sharks that patrol the waters offshore. From Jenner, Highway One struggles over the shoulders of steep mountains, where grazing cows have million-dollar views. After about fifteen miles you come to Fort Ross.

Fort Ross was built in 1812 by Russians who came to hunt sea otters along California's wildlife-rich coastline. The fort seems nearly as isolated as it did more than one hundred and eighty years ago. Its wooden structures have been preserved and restored, and today it's a state park. "I think it's very similar to the way it once looked," says Bill Walton, a ranger at the fort. "There are a few modern intrusions, like power lines, but not too many."

Five restored buildings inhabit the park: the Barracks, the Chapel, the Kuskov House, and two blockhouses. The Rotchev

The Pacific at Jenner

House is one of only four original buildings known to exist which were built by Russians on what is now American soil (the other three are in Alaska).

Who were the people who came here? Did they want to make this a Russian colony? "This was strictly a business venture," explains Bill. "This fort was a corporate investment. We don't think the company that built it had intentions of staying in America. All they wanted to do was make money."

The buildings were organized as a fort because the Russians weren't sure of the reception they'd receive once they arrived in California. They knew the land was claimed by Spain and that native people along the coast might resent their presence. To ensure against surprises, the Russians were well-armed and they built the stockade walls fourteen feet thick.

In addition to the fort's impressive buildings, you'll find many interesting displays at the park. The Trade Room, which is located in the Kuskov House building, contains goods that were exchanged with Chinese merchants; otter and seal pelts were shipped to Canton and exchanged for tea, silk, leather items, and trade beads. There is also the weapons and powder storage area, and you can see many agricultural implements.

Just north of Fort Ross, the road leads to spectacular Salt Point State Park, which rambles from a 1,500-foot ridgeline down to a craggy water's edge. Salt Point State Park is pretty large—it covers about fifteen miles of coastline. Ranger Dan Murley works in the park, and he can go often about his business and see very few other people, except perhaps some divers in the protected waters of the park's Gerstle Cove. Your only companions may be opportunistic gulls, or some easygoing seals doing what they do best—hanging out.

Dan enjoys leading people to one of the most bizarre parts of Salt Point—a coastal landscape that looks like something you'd find on the moon. "These unique formations were formed by a combination of the surf, the salt, wind, sand," he says.

Dan lives on the park grounds. Though there are no other houses nearby, he still feels he's part of a community. "You know," says Dan gazing out across the park, "when you look out the window and you see raccoons or brush rabbits or Sonoma County chipmunks or circling osprey or other birds, you realize this is your neighborhood and those are your neighbors. It's a wonderful feeling."

During the next forty miles northward

you'll come across a rhododendron reserve, Stewarts Point, Sea Ranch, and Anchor Bay, while you're marveling at the sheer physical beauty nature presents along the way. Eventually you'll land in a welcoming neighborhood of the human variety—the unspoiled town of Point Arena. As one local likes to put it, "This place is not quaint enough to crack your camera lens, and yet it's pleasant enough to stop and spend a day or two."

Point Arena is not gussied up for tourism. It feels like a real town, and two of its very real people are Jim Levine and his wife Alix. They moved to Mendocino County in the early 1970s to live on a commune. The commune is long gone, but they're still here in Point Arena.

Community is one reason Jim and Alix came here in the first place, but soon they fell in love with the ever-changing scenery. "It's green one minute, then it's blue—depending on the sun and the clouds—the color of the ocean is always different. We see it every day," comments Jim, "and it's something I wouldn't want to miss."

Just north of Point Arena is a lighthouse by the same name, built after an older lighthouse badly damaged by the 1906 earthquake was torn down. It is a good place to visit for a tour.

Ron Frame is a docent at the lighthouse and a retired police officer from Sacramento. When he first moved to the coast, he had no particular interest in lighthouses. Now you can't keep him away. "I've been a docent out here for three years," says Ron, "and I still bring my camera with me. People say, 'But you've taken pictures of every possible thing there is to take pictures of.' And I say, 'No, it changes daily.' Everything changes—it's part of the charm of this place."

There is a sweeping view from the top of the lighthouse. On clear days, Ron says with a wink, he can see the highrise hotels on Waikiki. In fact, this is the closest point to Hawaii in the lower forty-eight states.

Jenner Chamber of Commerce and
   Visitors Bureau 707-865-9433
Fort Ross State Historic Park
   707-847-3286
Salt Point State Park 707-847-3221
Point Arena Lighthouse 707-882-2777

Left: Point Arena; above: Fort Ross State Historic Park

THE DRIVE TO STEWARTS POINT:
Exploring the Backroads of Northern Sonoma County

There are plenty of bends, hills, and surprises along a narrow backroad in Sonoma County. From the wine country and the Russian River to a craggy coastline, it corkscrews through thirty-seven miles of delightful scenery. The twisting road passes no large towns but does skirt a big new lake, follows an inviting river, and finds its way through a dark redwood forest to some colorful characters. Along the route, the way things used to be comes to life at one of the oldest stores in California and one of the smallest post offices in North America.

The journey starts in the gentle wine country near Healdsburg on Highway 101, sixty-five miles north of San Francisco in Sonoma County. Follow Dry Creek Road northward, and in a few miles you can turn west on the old Skaggs Springs Stewarts Point Road.

The first major landmark is the massive Warm Springs Dam, some three thousand feet across and three hundred feet high. It looms above the nearby vineyards and forms Lake Sonoma. Ranger Sue Wilson works at the visitors center beneath the dam. "There are so many things for people to do here," says Sue. "We have facilities for boaters; you can camp out on the lake and on the shoreline also." Up on a hill above the lake are commanding views of the surrounding country and an easy self-guided nature trail through the woods. You see wildlife everywhere—on the wing and in the water. You can even go indoors next to the center and observe a state-of-the-art fish hatchery.

Continuing westward, as you leave Lake Sonoma on the Skaggs Springs Stewarts Point Road, you climb through grassy hillsides studded with oaks and manzanita and a little bit of history. It's hard to imagine that this meandering blacktop was ever busy, but back in the 1860s the Skaggs Springs Resort was just off the road, and it was one of the largest resorts in Northern California. People came here by the wagonload. After the resort closed during the Depression, this became a quiet byway.

The narrowing road reveals shifting scenery: wide vistas open up, and the Gualala River flows alongside your path for a while. Near the end of the drive west, redwoods close in, and the temperature begins to drop. Then suddenly, you

Lake Sonoma

Arch Richardson at the Stewarts Point Store

break through the trees and arrive on the coast at Stewarts Point.

The trip here from Healdsburg is very beautiful, but it's windy and takes a few hours. If you're wondering if it's worth the effort, you'll have no second guesses when you reach the coast—it's eye-popping. The shoreline at Stewarts Point is California at its untamed best: rocky bluffs towering over countless coves and inlets, an endless ocean, and hundreds of seabirds flying overhead.

Stewarts Point was once a lively logging port. Today just a handful of people call this place home. You'll find an abandoned saloon, an old garage, and some rusted logging equipment—remnants of another era.

There is still one thriving business though, the historic Stewarts Point Store, which has graced the shore here for well over a century. Somewhere between the oxen yokes, the Chinese wheelbarrow and gag gifts, you'll find the groceries and supplies for the people who live on this stretch of coast.

The old town of Stewarts Point might be gone, but the pioneers' self-sufficiency and camaraderie still survive at the store. Arch Richardson is the great-grandson of the store's original proprietor. "There have probably been more acquaintances and friendships made on this store's porch than any one place on this whole coast," says Arch. "It's just as good as a bar to meet people, but here you're going to meet someone who can talk sensible!"

The store is the perfect spot to fill up on local lore and fuel for the return trip. But before heading home, drive northward about four miles along the ocean's edge, then turn inland on Annapolis Road. You won't find a Naval Academy here, but you will find one of the smallest post offices anywhere.

"Actually it's not *the* smallest in the United States, but definitely in the top ten of the smallest," says postal clerk Rae Brodjeski. "I always have the coffee pot on in the winter, and the rocking chair in the small lobby is well-used. And I've weighed many a baby on my slider bar scale." This post office may not be the smallest, but it is perhaps the friendliest.

Skaggs Springs Stewarts Point is a classic backroad. It refuses to be rushed. It brings us to the welcoming porches of stores that give as much as they sell, and to post offices that gather memories as well as mail. It's a place—and a life—the way it used to be.

Lake Sonoma Visitors Center
707-963-3601
Stewarts Point Store 707-785-2406
Annapolis Post Office 707-886-5151

The Sierra Nevada and the Sacramento Valley

From left: Tufa towers at Mono Lake
and Devil's Postpile (both Tour 15)

9 GRAY LODGE WILDLIFE AREA:
The Central Valley's Haven for Birds— and Bird Lovers

Red-winged blackbirds, Gray Lodge Wildlife Area

If you venture out to one of the Central Valley's wildlife refuges in the wintertime you're bound to find some spectacular scenes. One favorite destination of the Backroads crew is the Gray Lodge Wildlife Area, managed by the California Department of Fish and Game. Gray Lodge is about three hours northeast of San Francisco, off Highway 99 west of the town of Gridley—the "Kiwi Capital of North America." Just look for the prominent signs along the highway near Gridley.

Bay Area naturalist Michael Ellis (whom we met in the Klamath Basin) leads nature trips all over the world, but the 8,400-acre Gray Lodge Wildlife Area is one of his favorite places. For him, a trip there is like a pilgrimage—and he loves to take people along.

"Some people go to the mountains or to the deserts or to the seashore, but I like coming here to listen to all the sounds of the waterfowl. And the views out here are always different in the wintertime. Sometimes there's heavy fog. Sometimes it's a crystalline blue day. Sometimes

it's raining. But it's *always* beautiful."

The most impressive thing about Gray Lodge and the other refuges in the valley is the sheer quantity of birds you'll see. If you visit during the winter, you'll probably be sharing Gray Lodge with a hundred thousand geese, and more than a million ducks! Sometimes the sky is actually darkened because there are so many birds in the air.

Michael's favorite thing to do out here is to wait until a whole flock of geese rises up out of the fields and flies overhead. Then he just sits, puts his binoculars down, cups his ears, and listens to the symphony of geese pass by.

Believe it or not, however, one of the best ways to look at the geese is to simply drive through the refuge and stay in your car. Once a car stops and people open doors and step out, the birds tend to get disturbed and fly away. Your car can act like a type of moving blind, and bird-watching from the warmth of your car makes for a good activity on those winter days when it's very cold or rainy.

So don't let bad weather keep you away—the birds will still be here. But if you want to stretch your legs, there are several nice hiking trails at Gray Lodge. There's also a wheelchair-accessible observation deck. Although you can see birds all day at Gray Lodge, they are most active in the early morning and late in the day as they move between feeding areas.

Birdwatchers can find everything in and around Gray Lodge from scads of coots to rare sandhill cranes. Sandhill cranes migrate south from their nesting grounds in Alaska to winter throughout the Central Valley. For Michael, cranes are particularly fascinating. "There's something so magnificent about seeing cranes wheel around in the sky and hearing their calls, which can carry more than a mile, thanks to their wonderful French horn–shaped trachea," he explains. "Sometimes they just drop down out of the fog like some ethereal ghost into a field. It's indescribable."

The best places to spot these leggy birds are fallow agricultural fields. And they tend to be devoted to favorite fields year after year. "During the wintertime the Central Valley is the place to be to see this tremendous concentration of waterfowl," says Michael. The Gray Lodge Wildlife Area serves up a wildlife spectacle every winter; it also gives you a glimpse of Central Valley life as it was about a hundred and fifty years ago.

Gray Lodge Wildlife Area 530-846-5176
Michael Ellis's Footloose Forays
  707-829-1844

Gray Lodge Wildlife Area

SUTTER BUTTES:
California's Middle Mountain

The Sacramento Valley is home to a place that has intrigued local residents and visitors alike for a long time—the Sutter Buttes. Surrounded by some five thousand square miles of extremely flat land, the Buttes are hard to miss as you are zooming up or down nearby Interstate 5. But missing the Sutter Buttes is exactly what most people do.

The Sutter Buttes are about three hours northeast of San Francisco, or about forty-five miles due north of Sacramento as the crow flies. To reach them, travel on Highway 20 to the middle of the valley via Highway 99 and Marysville and Yuba City in the east, or from Interstate 5 and Williams and Colusa in the west.

Visiting the Sutter Buttes requires a little advance planning because the Buttes are privately owned. But an organization called the Middle Mountain Foundation was set up to bring people to the Buttes and to help preserve this unique landscape as agricultural open space.

The Buttes are a cluster of volcanic domes that were formed more than a million years ago in the middle of the valley.

This circular set of peaks and valleys is about ten miles across. Three peaks make up the Buttes, and the tallest—South Butte—rises to approximately 2,100 feet. From the higher elevations of the Buttes the views are spectacular. On a clear day, you can even see Lassen Peak, more than seventy miles to the north.

The Buttes have carried many names over the years: Los Tres Picos, Marysville Buttes, and even the Sacramento Buttes. But for many tribes of Native Americans who lived in the valley the Buttes had a spiritual name. They called this volcano "middle mountain" because they considered the Buttes to be the center of the world—the place from which everything else grew.

The tribes didn't have permanent villages in the Buttes, but at least two tribes—the Maidu and the Patwin—maintained seasonal campsites here. The Indians came here, in part, to harvest the acorns of the blue oak and the live oak. They hulled and ground the acorns to prepare them for eating. The grinding holes the Indians used are still there.

Ira Heinrich is the former director of the Middle Mountain Foundation. He grew up around here, and the Buttes became his "middle mountain" too. "It's interesting," says Ira, "people come out here very excited and with a recreational perspective, and then, as the trip progresses, they fall

Sutter Buttes

into a contented, contemplative, heartfelt quietude. Someone asked me one time if I didn't envision myself as a guardian of the Buttes and I said, 'Absolutely not! It's the other way around.' This place guards me."

You'll drive through several working ranches on your way toward the top of the Buttes. Often with an area this beautiful, conservationists and ranchers struggle for control of the land and its uses. But in this case, nearly everyone is on the same side. Most of the property owners here recognize that the Buttes are special and need to be maintained. It's through their generosity and their public spirit that the Middle Mountain Foundation's interpretive access program can continue.

The foundation offers several ways to visit the Buttes. Open days are trips that anyone can sign up for. Each has a particular focus, like natural history, Native American tradition, or geology. If you put together at least ten people, you can arrange a charter trip to suit your interests. School groups of twenty or more are also encouraged. It's an excellent way to visit a little-known but highly visible part of California while helping to protect it well into the future.

Middle Mountain Foundation
530-634-6387

Sutter Buttes

DIGGING AROUND IN CALIFORNIA'S GOLD COUNTRY:
Nevada City, Malakoff Diggins, and Downieville

In the canyons and along the riverbanks of the Sierra Nevada foothills, a precious metal was discovered glittering in the bright California sun more than one hundred and fifty years ago. The discovery changed the state forever. Beginning in 1848, gold fever swept California like wildfire. Mining camps and entire cities sprung up overnight across the forested western slope of the Sierra as hordes of miners from around the world made the difficult trek to find their fortune and a new life. Today, the Gold Rush miners are gone, but their marks remain on the land and beneath it. Their legacy also survives in the many towns throughout California's Mother Lode, and their attitudes are still embodied in many of the area's residents.

To begin your exploration of the northern portion of the gold country set your sights on the city of Auburn just off Interstate 80. It's about a three-hour trip northeast of San Francisco. Once in Auburn—just as you begin the long climb

Empire Mine State Historic Park

up into the foothills—turn north on Highway 49 to Empire Mine State Historic Park and Nevada City. Later, you can continue on to Malakoff Diggins State Historic Park and the little town of Downieville.

As you approach Nevada City, you'll see a sign for the Empire Mine. Turn off the highway and work your way over to the state historic park. An important part of California's mining history lies underground here—a complex network of dark tunnels. The Empire Mine was a deep shaft mine and it operated from 1850 to 1956. During its long history the Empire Mine became one of the state's richest operations. Records show that some 5.8

million ounces of gold were removed from the Empire.

These days the mine is open to everyone, and just one of the many committed docents who love to show people around is Evelyn Bouchard. Evelyn helps people understand how the mining operation worked and what life was like for the miners. With the help of docents and interpretive signs you can learn that miners from Cornwall, England, were brought here to search thousands of feet deep for gold. They had the experience needed to dig an estimated 367 miles of tunnels in cramped, pitch-black quarters. "I can't imagine how they worked in those tight

little spaces," says Evelyn, still amazed after all her years of leading tours. "They had very little lighting."

While the miners worked below ground for little money, the mine owners enjoyed sunny elegance above ground— just next door but a world away. Today you can visit the owner's mansion and beautifully landscaped property adjacent to the old mine, but if a miner ever walked on these premises he would have been fired.

When you come back up for fresh air from the amazing tunnels of the Empire Mine, return to Highway 49 and continue into the foothills a few miles to Nevada City. You can still find horse-drawn carriages rolling through town past fine old buildings. There is also an impressive assortment of places to eat and stay. In Nevada City, yesterday and today have found a comfortable fit.

Just one of the many beautiful buildings in town is the National Hotel. It opened in 1856 and some claim it's the oldest operating hotel in the West. Gold Rush–era notables once stayed here, such as the stage star Lotta Crabtree and the stage robber Black Bart (he relieved an estimated twenty-eight Wells Fargo stagecoaches of their riches).

While the Gold Rush has subsided, gold fever has not. Local resident and former town mayor Pat Dyer trades in gold and jewelry in today's Nevada City.

Mine tunnel at the Empire Mine

"Even today we could have people walk in here in their grubbies with anywhere from $10 worth of gold to $1,000 worth of gold to sell."

But as gold became more scarce and less profitable to mine, the town's businesses began to suffer. "But the beauty of that is that the town was left unremodeled," Pat says. Many of the buildings here are now preserved on the National Registry of Historic Places, and visitors love to come and see them.

If you continue into the mountains from Nevada City on North Bloomfield Road you can see how some of the gold mining in the Sierra Nevada was done in broad daylight. Malakoff Diggins State Park in the "town" of North Bloomfield, once called Humbug by unlucky miners, is an impressive example. More than one hundred years ago, there were fifteen hundred people living here. Today, the population is three. Ranger Ken Hue is one of those residents.

As Ken points out, the town is a tame reminder of its former self. "The building we use today as our museum was a saloon," says Ken. "Three doors down was another saloon. Across the street from that was a saloon and next to that was yet another saloon. So, you get an idea of what life was like here."

Thirsts were washed away by spirits, and the gold nearby was washed away by water. From 1853 to 1884, miners blasted hillsides with huge water cannons, turning soil and rock into mud and gravel from which the gold was extracted. "If you dug a tunnel six feet in diameter from Los Angeles to New York, that would be how much dirt they moved," says Ken. But the cannons finally stopped when the mining became too destructive and unprofitable. What was once the richest hydraulic mine in the world is now a colorful scar softened by nature's healing hand.

Work your way north of Malakoff Diggins and you'll reunite with Highway 49. Here, the beautiful roadway follows the swift water of the Yuba River's north fork. Eventually the road leads into a picturesque town that almost squeezes the highway to a halt. It's Downieville, an authentic relic of the Gold Rush teeming with tales and characters to tell them.

Don Russell is the latest editor of the *Mountain Messenger*, Downieville's hometown newspaper. "This place was a classic rip-roaring, wide-open, mining camp," laughs Don, who continues with an explanation of his editorial policies. "There aren't enough facts to go around here, so I just started putting my opinions up front and writing outrageously slanted stories." It is a hallowed tradition here in Downieville, practiced by one of the

The National Hotel, Nevada City

Malakoff Diggins State Historic Park

Messenger's earliest reporters, Mark Twain.

Today folks come to Downieville to fish, bicycle, and soak up local lore. The town is full of history. It's also full of something else—good humor. "We believe in California history," says Don. "We believe in it so much that we make it up every day!" The best thing about Downieville is its friendly people. Hang out for a little bit and you're likely to meet most of them. Downieville might have been built on nineteenth-century gold, but it survives on twentieth-century humor and hospitality.

Empire Mine State Historic Park
530-273-8522
Nevada City Chamber of Commerce
530-265-2692
Malakoff Diggins State Historic Park
530-265-2740

TAHOE UNTAMED:
From Winter Outings
to the Wild West

Mark Twain once called Tahoe the "Lake in the Sky." At 6,200 feet above sea level, and surrounded by a halo of snow-capped Sierran peaks, Lake Tahoe does in fact look as though is it floating in the heavens. Not only is Lake Tahoe high, but its deep blue water makes it seem bottomless. Compared to most of the world's lakes, it practically is—its deepest reaches have been measured 1,648 feet below the lake's shimmering surface.

Lake Tahoe is nestled in the Sierra Nevada some two hundred miles east of San Francisco, about a four-hour drive. Interstate 80 leads to the north shore of the lake while Highway 50 is the most direct route to the south shore. The California-Nevada border runs roughly north-south down the middle of this Sierra gem.

To many people Lake Tahoe in winter means downhill skiing and casino gambling. More than a dozen ski resorts are

Fallen Leaf Lake (foreground) and Lake Tahoe from Angora Lookout

here, where the relatively new sport of snowboarding is also wildly popular. And on the Nevada side of the lake there are plenty of casinos, especially in South Lake Tahoe.

But there are less expensive ways to enjoy the lake during the winter and still have a great time. One way is to simply drive around the lake; it's about a three-hour drive. But it will take longer—and it should—if you stop to take in the scenic views and stretch your legs. There are also snow parks around the perimeter where you can go sledding or rent a plastic saucer and scoot downhill. You can also get out on the water on a paddlewheel boat, or go riding behind a one-horse open sleigh. Or you can simply walk down a beach and have it practically all to yourself.

If you'd like to get out on your own, one special way of pursuing some solo winter activity (OK, maybe there will be a *few* other people) is cross-country skiing along the quiet shore of Emerald Bay, a state park on the west side of Lake Tahoe.

State Park Ranger Bob Burke leads free cross-country trips into the park during the winter. "I've been up here more than fifteen years," says Bob, "and I'm still not tired of the view out over Emerald Bay." If you're really lucky on one of Ranger Burke's free skiing trips, you'll see bald eagles who spend the winter in this region.

"It's a whole different mood here in the winter," says Bob. "If you've visited in the summertime you'll know there are a lot of people and lots of boats on the water. In the winter there are practically no boats and hardly any other person in sight."

The cross-country ski trips into the park are only moderately strenuous, and they lead, as does a one-mile hiking trail, to an important landmark next to Emerald Bay—Vikingsholm. Vikingsholm is a massive house built in 1928 by Laura Josephine Knight. Her travels through Scandinavia influenced her design of the building. Today it's considered one of the finest examples of Scandinavian architecture in the United States.

After a visit to see Vikingsholm (the house is open in summer for tours) you can explore some of the paths climbing upslope around the bay. A few tables along the way make for good spots to stop and rest, have a snack, and take in the spectacular view. The island you see in the middle of the bay has a small tea-house, where Mrs. Night would entertain guests on warm summer afternoons.

The Lake Tahoe region is a great winter escape for people of all ages, abilities, and tastes. But if you want to break away and go someplace really different, drive east a few miles into the hills of Nevada. You'll find the Wild West still alive and well in the town of Virginia City.

The scenery changes from high-Sierra woods to Big Basin sagebrush and juniper pines as you travel. One favorite route

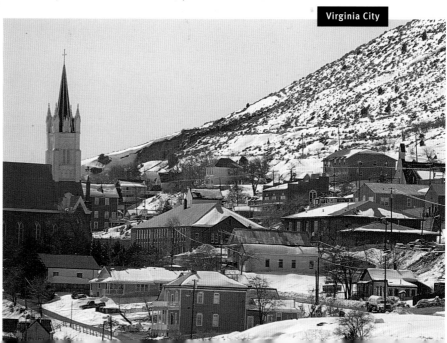

Virginia City

Eagle Falls, near Emerald Bay

from South Lake Tahoe into Nevada is along the Kingsbury Grade. It's the old Pony Express and stagecoach route. You'll pass the Nevada state capital in Carson City.

As you approach Virginia City, you'll see some of the old Comstock mining operations that once attracted more than twenty-two thousand fortune seekers and made Virginia City "the richest place on earth." In the late 1800s, more gold and silver was mined here than any-where else in the world—some $400 million worth.

Today the town depends on tourism for its livelihood. Its current population of nine hundred plays host to a million and a half visitors a year. Local range-manage-ment officer John Tyson explains, "Virginia City is not a Disneyland. What you see is what you get. We are as authentic as the day this town was founded in 1859." Many of the town's buildings date from the 1870s, and there are some twenty cemeteries.

Another relic from the past is a net-work of mining tunnels that add up to about seven hundred miles of under-ground passages. You can check these out at the old Chollar Mine. It operated from 1861 until the 1970s. Now it's open for tours May through October. It's exactly the way it was when the miners worked in here for $4 a day, twenty-four hours a day.

From the toil of massive mining operations grew a city that was once among the most advanced in the West. One indication of Virginia City's wealth and advancement is evident in the old Fourth Ward School, now a museum. It was one of the first buildings in the West to have central heating and indoor plumbing.

If you come to Virginia City during the warm months, you can ride on the railroad tracks around town behind a real steam locomotive. Trains operate daily Memorial Day through September, and on weekends in October. It's a nice leisurely trip, just like it was in 1876 when President Grant rode the same rails on a visit.

There are plenty of things to do in Virginia City even in the off-season. The place has several small museums, and there are some nice walking and driving tours you can take with knowledgeable guides. And, it's hard to resist taking a peek at the infamous "suicide table" in the Delta Saloon, or whetting your whistle at the old Bucket of Blood Saloon. "Virginia City had great character," says an obviously proud John Tyson, "and it still does."

Emerald Bay State Park 530-525-7277
Comstock History Museum,
   Golden Eagle Tours 702-847-0678

ALPINE COUNTY:
A Secret Winter
Wonderland

Alpine County is the least populated and one of the wildest counties in all California. It's a place where mountains and meadows seem to outnumber men and women. Remarkably, this secret playground is just over the mountains from the hustle and bustle of South Lake Tahoe.

Alpine County was at its peak in population and economic well-being when it was created in 1864. These days, it's about as unpopulated as it's ever been.

At last count, there were just more than one thousand people living there.

Alpine County is also a perfect place to visit for rest and relaxation or recreation and exercise. Although this mountainous county is a perfect destination year-round, it is especially beautiful when draped with a winter coat of snow.

Alpine County is about a four-hour drive east from the Bay Area. You can follow two main routes: Highway 88 past Jackson in the Gold Country, or Highway 50 to South Lake Tahoe, then south on Highway 89.

Today's Alpine County is mostly National Forest lands and wilderness

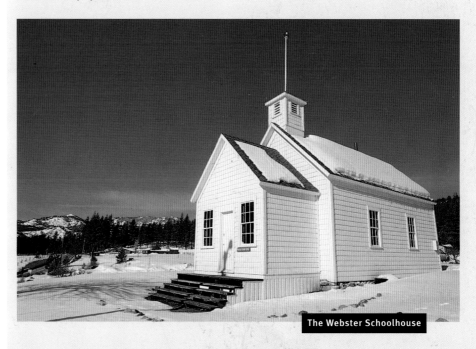

The Webster Schoolhouse

Sorensen's

areas. It has no supermarkets, no traffic signals, and no practicing doctors or dentists. But it does have a county seat—the town of Markleeville. Traffic in Markleeville typically consists of two guys hanging out on the road, especially during the wintertime. "The most embarrassing thing in the world would be to get hit by a car in Markleeville," laughs Bob Rudden, owner of the Markleeville General Store. According to Bob, Markleeville once had a population of some two thou-

sand people. Now its population is less than two hundred.

Markleeville was built mostly by miners and loggers. But the region's human history goes back much further than the 1860s, says Nancy Thornburg, who runs the Alpine County Museum in Markleeville (open Memorial Day through October), which has an impressive collection for such a sparsely populated area. Nancy says that the Washoe Indians were the earliest settlers here. At the museum you can see a Washoe projectile point

that's nearly ten thousand years old. The museum even has its own nineteenth-century jail and the Webster School-house, which was built in 1882 by the people of Markleeville on the top of a hill overlooking town.

Just north of town, close to the junction of Highways 88 and 89, you'll find a low-key resort in a grove of pines and aspen. Sorensen's is a place that reflects the region's rustic qualities. The resort has been a haven for travelers since the 1920s, when Martin and Irene Sorensen first started renting out cabins for seventy-five cents a night.

The Sorensens are gone now, but their nurturing ways thrive in the resort's current owners, John and Patty Brissenden. "Our mission statement," says John, "is to revive and renew the spirit of our guests. And the land does much of it for us." Sorensen's welcomes kids and their families, and pets if they are well-behaved. There are a variety of cabins in various sizes, shapes, and prices. And the food is excellent.

For many decades, Sorensen's closed during the long and snowy winter months. But not anymore. These days Sorensen's—and much of Alpine County—is nirvana for both seasoned and beginning cross-country skiers. During the winter, Hope Valley Cross Country operates out of the resort. Hope Valley's friendly instructors, and the gentle landscape, will get you up and skiing in no time. There is something for every kind of skier here—from flat-meadow skiing to more challenging routes.

Alpine County also provides one of the most delightful winter activities imaginable: dog sledding. Once you hunker down under some blankets and the dogs get going, the ride is remarkably quiet and smooth, and often fast. It's a wonderful way to take in the region's spectacular scenery. Dotty Dennis, who has been mushing for more than twenty years, runs

Husky Express. "My dogs just love this work," says Dotty. The sleds hold two adults and one or two small children, and the rides are reasonably priced. You can also pet the friendly dogs after your ride.

In many ways, Alpine County is the result of impressive geological activity. Geologic forces created the rugged mountains, and they've spawned some therapeutic hot springs along the way. If you'd like to unwind after a day of adventure in the high country try Grover Hot Springs, northwest of Markleeville at the end of the appropriately named Hot Springs Road. The low price of admission is as comforting as the water and the views from the swimming pools (one hot, one cold) are unbeatable. Here—and virtually wherever you go or whatever you do in Alpine County—you're rarely far from the natural world and countless recreational opportunities.

Alpine County Museum 530-694-2317
Sorensen's Resort 800-423-9949
Hope Valley Cross Country
    530-694-2266
Husky Express dog sled tours
    702-782-3047
Grover Hot Springs State Park
    530-694-2249
Alpine County Chamber of Commerce
    530-694-2475

Husky Express

41

*Between October March
+ ~~December~~*

THE COSUMNES RIVER:
A Wild Side of
the Central Valley

The Cosumnes River

Just over the eastern hills of the Bay Area is a place many people drive through as quickly as possible—the Great Central Valley. Nowadays, much of it looks like one, ongoing farm field amid newly sprawling cities and towns, but that wasn't always the case. Even today, there is still some wilderness here, and much of it is very easy to visit. In the Central Valley you can find slow-moving rivers bordered by dense forests, wetlands, and lots of wildlife. You can also find important tracts of land being restored for California's future.

Riparian, or streamside, forests once meandered alongside virtually every river in the Central Valley. But today, with the explosion of development in California, only about 4 percent of the state's riparian forests remain. One of the best places to see this fertile yet rare habitat is at the twelve-thousand-acre Cosumnes River Preserve, twenty miles south of Sacramento on Interstate 5, then immediately east on Twin Cities Road.

The Cosumnes River Preserve is home to California's largest remaining valley oak riparian forest. The preserve also protects thousands of acres of wetlands and is home to the Cosumnes, the only river

which cascades undammed off the Sierra Nevada. Within this splendid combination of habitats, only minutes south of Sacramento, some two hundred species of birds have been recorded, including numerous migratory species.

Although a visit to the preserve is fantastic any time of the year, between October and March you can see thousands of ducks and geese in the preserve's wetlands, and hundreds of sandhill cranes high-stepping through adjacent native grasslands and across fallow croplands.

The preserve is a joint venture of the Nature Conservancy, Ducks Unlimited, the Federal Bureau of Land Management, the California Department of Fish and Game, and the Sacramento County Parks and Recreation Department. Says former preserve manager Greg Elliot, "We have

what's probably the best remaining example of this ecological community left in the world right here."

Although the preserve is managed by professionals, it receives some of its most valuable assistance from volunteers, like retired farmers Dolph Lahman and Art Fritzer. These former sportsmen became concerned about the region's declining population of wood ducks and decided to do something about it. "Wood ducks are cavity nesters," explains Greg, "kind of like spotted owls, and because there aren't a lot of big old trees with cavities left in them, that's one of the main limiting factors on their numbers."

The wood ducks were so desperate for proper nesting sites several years back that they were trying to wriggle their way through the knotholes in Art's barn. So he began a nest-box building program to create artificial cavities for the ducks—and leave the barn for the resident barn owls. The first year Art put up twelve boxes; nine were used as nests. Now, under Art and Dolph's watchful eyes, there are well over three hundred nest boxes on or near the preserve, and the population of wood ducks is increasing. There are some five thousand wood duck boxes scattered up and down the Central Valley, all based on the preserve's successful efforts. "I want to help these and other birds now rather than hunt them,"

says Art. "I get a kick out of *my* birds."

Dolph agrees. "If you're a hunter and fisherman," says Dolph, "we feel that you should give back some of what you took—for the next generation of young people. And that's what we're doing."

There's more to the Cosumnes River Preserve than ducks and geese, of course. The heart of the preserve, the river, is unusual because every winter the lower Cosumnes River is allowed to do something it's been doing for eons—flood. When the river floods the water spreads over vast areas of the preserve, depositing silt and enriching the riparian

forest. Flooding also helps many riparian species colonize once-barren riverbanks and expand their range. During the peak of flooding as much as half of the preserve is underwater. In some places it's just a few inches of water, but in others it can be five feet deep.

Although boating and canoe trips are a favorite activity at the preserve, you can also go hiking. The Willow Slough Trail, a three-mile path, takes you through just about every habitat here, including bird-packed wetlands—both natural and restored—along the river. There is also a new visitor center (on Franklin Boulevard) packed with information and hands-on exhibits for kids. The visitor center is a good place to start your visit.

The possibilities seem to be endless along this slow-moving river: you can come out to the preserve to experience a slice of the Central Valley as it once was. You can work as a volunteer doing everything from building nesting boxes to planting oak trees, with your family, friends, or co-workers. The exciting work being done at Cosumnes—by both professionals and volunteers—is helping ensure that generations of wildlife and humans thrive here well into the future.

Cosumnes River Preserve 916-684-2816
Nature Conservancy 415-777-0487

The Willow Slough Trail

TIOGA PASS, MONO LAKE, AND MAMMOTH LAKES:
Across the Sierra to an Inland Sea and Beyond

When most Californians think about mountains they conjure up images of the Sierra—John Muir's "Range of Light." The Sierra is a mountain wonderland, a universe apart from other regions of the state.

One wonderful way to cross the Sierra is Tioga Pass Road, one of the most scenic drives anywhere in the world, and just about as high as you can drive in California. It's a roadway that leads into a landscape of spectacular geological formations, crystal clear light, and grand adventures on the Sierra's east side.

Tioga Pass Road begins near the Big Oak Flat entrance to Yosemite National Park on Highway 120. From the Bay Area it's about a four-hour drive in the summer to this juncture. Once on Tioga (a continuation of Highway 120), you wriggle your way east across the park, ending up at Mono Lake and the town of Lee Vining.

Tioga is not a route to take if you're in a hurry, because you'll feel compelled to pull over at every viewpoint. You might see an irresistible waterfall cascading alongside the roadway or a deer grazing

Tenaya Lake, Yosemite National Park

by a lake, or you might want to go climb a rock. One of the most beautiful places to stop is Olmstead Point, just before Tuolumne Meadows. This spectacular turnout gives you a real feeling for the high country—it's all air, distance, and granite. You also get an unusual view of Half Dome down in Yosemite Valley.

Several miles east of Olmstead Point is Tuolumne Meadows, in the heart of the Sierra. During the summer, tent cabins and campsites are available here, and it's also a very popular spot from which to head out for the high country on horse-back or by backpacking.

It was the lands around Tuolumne Meadows, more than any other, that inspired John Muir to lead the fight to protect Yosemite's high country. Here, after watching the sun illuminating nearby mountains, he nicknamed the Sierra "the Range of Light."

According to Bruce Brossman of the Yosemite Mountaineering School, the country encircling Tuolumne Meadows is a major rock-climbing area in its own right. "It's overshadowed somewhat by Yosemite Valley," says Bruce. "But if this was anywhere else it would be an extremely famous rock-climbing area."

Back on Tioga Road, heading east from Tuolumne, you slowly climb to Tioga Pass at nearly ten thousand feet. The mountains to the north and south of the

Devil's Postpile

pass rise to thirteen thousand feet. Tioga is closed in the winter and in heavy snow years it can stay blocked as late as July.

From the rangers station at the park's boundary you plunge downhill into sage-brush country. Descending a mountain pass can be slightly depressing, because of the high country beauty you are leaving behind, but not on this drive. You drop right into the mysterious realm of Mono Lake—a wounded inland sea on the mend—and the town of Lee Vining along its western shore.

Mono Lake is truly otherworldly. The tufa towers found mostly on the southern edge of the lake look like something out of a science fiction movie. They form when calcium from freshwater springs reacts with carbonates in the mineral-rich lake water—which is three times saltier than the Pacific. You can see these tufas because in 1941 the thirsty city of Los Angeles began diverting water from Mono Lake's freshwater tributaries. Since then, the lake has lost half its volume, exposing the forests of tufa in the process.

According to Stacey Simon, this may be the lowest we'll ever see Mono Lake. Stacey works for the Mono Lake Committee, formed by concerned people who want to save the lake. "Many people recognize its ecological significance," explains Stacey, "especially people who love birds."

Mono Lake is the nesting ground for 85 percent of the state's California gulls. Millions of migratory birds stop here as well, such as Wilson's phalaropes, American avocets, and eared grebes. There are no fish in the lake, but a unique species of brine shrimp provides an abundant source of food for the birds.

After a long uphill struggle for the Mono Lake Committee and countless other "Monophiles," the state water board recently ordered a halt to water diversions until the lake returns to its 1963 level. That may take twenty to thirty years,

Olmstead Point, Yosemite National Park

miles from Lee Vining—is the more sizable community of Mammoth Lakes, a gateway to the eastern Sierra. If you are venturing south to Mammoth, why not take a short detour through June Lake on Highway 158? It's a beautiful drive, and you can find things to do all year round: winter skiing, summer fishing, and in the fall, colors abound.

Once in Mammoth Lakes you'll realize the region is a perfect staging area for a multitude of activities: hiking, fishing, skiing, biking, horseback riding, and backpacking into the Sierra.

As you explore the Mammoth region you'll soon discover that there is no "mammoth" lake. Instead, there are six delicate lakes nearby—a cluster of alpine jewels. And of course, there's 11,053-foot Mammoth Mountain, which offers an incredible 360-degree panorama spanning two states. From Mammoth Mountain, you can gaze out at a vast and sparse landscape to the east, or you can look down upon inviting lakes and lush forests.

Mammoth is a world-class ski resort. In the summer, it becomes a world-class mountain biking area. Those who dare can haul their bikes up on the gondola, and then ride down the daunting Kamikaze Trail. Also, unlike the other stops on our journey, Mammoth Lakes has everything from outlet shopping to a wide range of restaurants, hotels, motels, and resorts.

but positive signs are already visible.

Mark Twain once called Mono the Dead Sea of California. There is a unique quality to the air and light at Mono Lake, and to the solitude and tranquility of the landscape. The spaces here on the edge of the Great Basin are so vast it's as if the light bends over the horizon, lifting up the Sierra's sharp-edged eastern escarpment and outlining it in exquisite detail. The lake's surface, described by one early scientist as "burnished metal," changes continuously.

Mono Lake is easy to explore. Flat trails lead you to the tufa towers at the south shore parking area and at the north shore's county park. There's a Forest Service visitors center with interpretive programs and a nature trail just north of downtown Lee Vining. The Mono Lake Committee has a first-class environmental bookstore right in town and conducts guided sunset walks and other activities. Lee Vining itself is a small outpost with a few motels, several restaurants, and places to buy groceries and gas.

Down Highway 395—about thirty

Mammoth Mountain is a volcano, though it hasn't erupted for fifty thousand years. The most unusual evidence of past activity here looks like the unfinished work of a highly skilled prehistoric stone-mason. It's called the Devil's Postpile, and today it's an eight-hundred-acre national monument, a few miles west of Mammoth.

The postpile was formed after an eruption of basalt lava filled the area. As the lava cooled, it also shrank, and seemingly symmetrical cracks appeared. A perfect combination of conditions caused the cracks to deepen, creating the columns we see today. In addition to the impressive geology, there is a campsite here and the headwaters of the San Joaquin River meander close by.

A visit to Mono and Mammoth lakes can renew visitors both physically and spiritually. Whether you decide to first turn left, or right, at the bottom of the spectacular Tioga Pass Road, you are bound to have a good time exploring the Sierra's eastern escarpment.

Yosemite Mountaineering School
209-372-8344
Mono Lake Committee 760-647-6595
Mammoth Lakes Visitors Bureau
760-934-2712
Devil's Postpile National Monument
760-934-2289

YOSEMITE IN WINTER:
From Culinary Delights to Tranquil Backcountry Skiing

If you love Yosemite National Park but have never seen it in winter, you should take the time to visit during that quiet and splendid time of year. During the winter, Yosemite puts on a different and maybe even more beautiful face. Nature seems to take the valley back to restore it. And being nearly alone in this quiet, cathedral-like granite valley is enchanting.

If you think there isn't much to do during the winter here, you couldn't be more wrong. You can go out on a cross-country ski trail and be mostly alone. The valley's hiking and snowshoe paths are uncrowded, you can downhill ski at

Yosemite Valley

Badger Pass without waiting in long lines, and rooms are actually available at the world-famous Ahwahnee Hotel, which hosts a series of amazing banquets to lure winter visitors.

After several snows in the park the Badger Pass ski season begins and the road to Glacier Point closes to cars. Luckily, it's open to Nordic skiers, and the trip up to the point is one of the most exciting things to experience in Yosemite. Dick Ewart and Vicki McMichael know the snowcovered trail to Glacier Point well. Dick is a Yosemite ranger and Vicki leads trips for the Yosemite Cross Country Ski School.

"The trip all the way to Glacier Point is ten and a half miles," explains Dick. He says beginners can't make it all the way there and back in a day, but they can go part way and still have a fantastic time. Skiers visiting with the cross-country school spend the night up near the point in a rustic cabin. It has bunk beds, food, a stove, and hot coffee.

Once you're at the point, the valley spreads out three thousand feet below through the clouds and winter mist. "I never get tired of the view from the point," says Vicki. "In the summer, visitors are lined up here. It's crowded. In the winter, with a bit of work, you can be up here all alone. And in the winter it really is a different place. The snow fills the cracks of the

Ice skaters at Curry Village

granite walls encircling the valley and the clouds rise right up from the valley floor."

Through the snow and fog from Glacier Point you can see a Yosemite landmark down in the valley: the Ahwahnee, one of America's most beautifully integrated examples of rustic architecture. It fits in well with Yosemite's overwhelming majesty, and it has been a warm and inviting place since 1927 to ordinary folks and famous names alike. Queen Elizabeth and Winston Churchill stayed here; so have many American presidents. In the early 1960s President Kennedy and the First Lady landed in a helicopter right out in front of the Ahwahnee and stayed in the Presidential Suite.

Jack Hicks has witnessed much of the Ahwahnee's history since he started working there in the 1950s. "Our lead time for reservations from April through October is a year and a day in advance. I think it was in 1987 when the Pope was visiting California that he made inquiries about coming to Yosemite and staying at the Ahwahnee. But when he found out there was such a large lead time for people to get in he didn't want to displace anybody, so he decided not to come to Yosemite. Even the Pope couldn't get in!"

It may be tough to get a room at the Ahwahnee during the peak season, but during the winter the Ahwahnee actually tries to attract visitors. One way is with

The Ahwahnee Hotel

the Chef's Holiday program. This annual event features several dozen guest chefs sharing their culinary secrets in the Great Lounge of the hotel. The program includes a reception and banquet in the dining hall.

Between the uncrowded skiing and hiking,and the roaring fires at the Ahwahnee, Yosemite can feel like home in the wintertime. But if you visit, there's a possibility that, like Dick Ewart, you may never leave. "At the time I figured three or four years, then I'd go to Zion and then I'd go to the Grand Canyon. But I fell in love with Yosemite, and I thought 'I'm already in heaven! How can I go anywhere else?'"

Ahwahnee Hotel 209-252-4848
Glacier Point Skiing, the Yosemite Cross
   Country Ski School 209-372-8444

North Bay

From left: Harbor seals near Bodega Bay (Tour 21),

Marin Headlands Visitors Center (Tour 24), and Sonoma Valley grapevines (Tour 20)

WESTSIDE ROAD:
Traveling the Sonoma County Farm Trails

Sonoma County is known for its farms, wineries, and rural atmosphere. Much of it looks the same as it did one hundred years ago, and that makes it an ideal weekend getaway. Here you can leave cities and suburbs behind and change gears, downshifting into a relaxing Sunday drive.

Westside Road leads to some of the best that Sonoma County has to offer, from giant horses to miniature grapevines, to small family farms and historic wineries. Along the way, the tastes, sights, and smells of the region's remarkable bounty spring from the land and are gladly shared by the people who work it.

Westside Road begins in Healdsburg, about one hour and fifteen minutes north of the Golden Gate Bridge on Highway 101. It winds south and west for some twelve miles near the Russian River, ending up outside the town of Guerneville.

Immediately outside of Healdsburg, the gentle landscape unfolds before you, and in spring it erupts into a rainbow of wildflowers. Down the road a little ways, jabbering geese and ducks greet you at Dragonfly Floral, a farm that specializes in flower arrangements. The flower shop is the brainchild of Bonnie Yuill-Thornton, and she welcomes visitors who call ahead. Bonnie grows all sorts of exotic flowers, including about four hundred varieties of roses.

Just a few hundred yards from Dragonfly Floral is a curious spot called Petite Vines. It doesn't look like much from the outside because most of its business is mail order. But inside, the greenhouses are packed with hundreds of bonsai grapevines. "In order to create these," explains Petite Vines' Keith Pratt, "we take a small cutting and we make it walk the walk of life or death. These plants are ideal for somebody who wants to own a piece of the wine country and see the plant go through the various seasonal changes, but who doesn't have twenty acres in the backyard."

About a mile and a half farther down Westside Road—past rows of normal-sized grapevines with gorgeous views—fresh organic produce beckons you at Middleton Farm. "We pick everything fresh," boasts Malcolm Skall. "We don't pick it and store it in the cold room. So what we have growing is what we'll have that day for sale. And half the time we'll go out and pick it in the field when you're here."

Westside Road runs through the Russian River wine district, home of several fine wineries. One of the most fasci-

Keith Pratt at Petite Vines

nating—Hop Kiln Winery—honors the fact that this was once beer country also. The kiln that dried hops for beer is now an unusual setting for tasting wine. It is also considered to be one of the best tasting rooms in California.

Hop Kiln's wines have also won many awards, much to the surprise of owner Marty Griffin. "I came from a teetotalling family and I bought this ranch back in 1961," says Marty. "It had these incredible old vineyards on it. I started making homemade wine, and it turned out so good that I eventually got into the wine business."

Marty is a retired doctor, and he's been an active environmentalist all his life. Decades ago, he was responsible for helping save Audubon Canyon Ranch and other parts of West Marin County from development. Now he's set aside part of his land along the Russian River as a preserve to maintain the character of the Westside Road area.

The beautiful scenery at Hop Kiln makes for a wonderful picnic spot, and the historic buildings harken back to a time gone by. That same feeling is alive one mile away at Westside Farms, first established in 1869. Current owners Pam and Ron Kaiser came here for a simpler life and continue to farm their land with draft horses. "We're kind of bringing back that tradition to this farm," says Ron, "so

Fresh produce at Middleton Farm

this way of life is known for another one hundred-plus years."

Westside Farms is only open to the public twice during the year: the last three weeks of October—when the place is awash in pumpkins, squash, and decorative corn—and in June for pick-your-own berries season. If you're lucky, Pam will have the horses hitched up and they will take you for a spin in an old-fashioned wooden wagon. And no visit to Westside Farms is complete without paying respects to Rosebud, the noisy one-thousand-pound pig!

Hearing Rosebud squeal, smelling fresh produce, and tasting great wine in a rustic setting are some of the simpler pleasures that make Westside Road a welcome respite from the hustle and bustle of city life. It's easy to see why all these denizens of Westside Road have fallen in love with this place, and why they love to share it with visitors.

On your way back to the Bay Area, consider stopping by an herb garden with an attitude—a whimsical attitude—just south of Santa Rosa, immediately west of Highway 101. The place is called Mom's Head, and it's part of the Sonoma County

Hop Kiln Winery

Farm Trails, a collection of more than one hundred small farms featuring everything from potbellied pigs to carnivorous plants.

Mom's Head and its eclectic assortment of plants and other items is the creation of Vivien Hillgrove and Karen Brocco. "Mom was a cat that we had for eighteen years," explains Vivien. "And we thought,

one day when we move to the country and we have a small estate—that's a joke—we would name it after Mom. Mom's head was so adorable from the back that we thought, 'Wouldn't it be cute to have Mom's Head as a logo for our place?'"

"We started this place because we were looking for herbs that we had read about in various books," explains Karen,

"but that we couldn't find. We thought that was ridiculous. Here we are in a beautiful county that can grow anything, and you can't find these herbs." A walk through their nursery reveals a stunning array of herbs, everything from lemon balm and mullen plant to agrimony. But they do more than collect, grow, and sell herbs. They also gather stories about plants from history such as sweet wood-ruff, which was once used during May festivals hundreds of years ago. They also have woad, an ancient plant used by the Druids to paint their bodies blue in England of yesteryear.

An unlikely pair of farmers, Vivien and Karen actually earn their livelihoods as motion-picture editors. Their credits include *Amadeus* and *The Right Stuff,* and they've worked with such filmmakers as Francis Ford Coppola, David Lynch, and Saul Zaentz. When they need to relax, Vivien and Karen can retreat to their Buffalo Gal Bar packed with eclectic items, or retreat to the Herb Reading Room inside a real caboose. Visitors are welcome from 11 A.M. to 5 P.M. on Sundays, from April to September. People are welcome in their reading room, but for now the caboose is not open to the public.

"We opened this place to the public so people can enjoy it as much as we do," says Vivien. "We just love these little plants, and we hope others will too."

Dragonfly Floral 707-433-3739
Petite Vines 707-433-6255
Middleton Farm 707-433-4755
Hop Kiln Winery 707-433-6491
Westside Farms 707-431-1432
Mom's Head 707-585-8575
Sonoma County Farm Trails 707-571-8288

SAFARI WEST:
A Bay Area African Safari

18

Around virtually every corner of the backroads you can find a surprise. For example, did you know that right beside a very busy road near Santa Rosa in Sonoma County you can actually take an African safari? At Safari West, you can view and photograph exotic animals as you might see them in Africa.

Safari West is also a breeding ground for many rare and endangered species, part of an international effort to save these animals from extinction. The sprawling grounds of Safari West are sixty-five miles north of San Francisco and about ten miles northeast of Santa Rosa off Mark West Springs Road.

Mike Farley is a naturalist who leads visitors on a two-hour car safari through the preserve's large enclosures, followed by a one-hour walking tour of the smaller areas. Mike used to work on wildlife films, and he likes the way Safari West creates a natural setting for the animals.

"What you'll see here is all normal behavior," says Mike, "breeding, defending their territories, everything. The animals wander around at will, and it's really

Watusi cattle at Safari West

nice to see them intermingle. *And* you can save the plane fare of going all the way to Africa!"

Tours at Safari West are not cheap, but it's quite a spectacular place. There are some animals here that you couldn't see even if you did go to Africa. The scimitar-horned oryx is thought to be extinct in the wild, but it's being successfully bred at Safari West and other U.S. parks and zoos in the hope that someday it can be reintroduced to its native North Africa.

One of the best things about Safari West is that you have to go and find the animals. With about a hundred acres in the main enclosure, they could be anywhere. One of the most impressive animals here is the Cape eland, among the largest of the world's antelopes. An adult male can weigh 2,200 pounds.

There is one exception to the normal animal behavior at Safari West—there's a sheep with a crush on an eland. "We have this little sheep from a neighboring ranch that fell in love with this female eland," explains Mike with a shrug, "and it stays by her side, everywhere she goes. Anytime we try and catch the little guy, he hides behind her, or it gets underneath the male eland where it knows we can't possibly get it. It even acts like an eland now. It'll flick its head from side to side if you get too close, and it charges other animals and tries to stick them with its horns but he doesn't have any. He's confused."

You'll also see bongo antelope, which originated deep in the Congo. They're among the gentlest animals at Safari West. "Notice the bongos have vertical stripes," says Mike. "The rule of thumb with antelope is if they have horizontal stripes, they live in the plains areas. If they have vertical stripes, they live in the jungles."

Just like on the real plains of Africa, the vehicle is the best place from which to view the wildlife at Safari West. The animals are used to it. While most aren't as gregarious as the bongos, they will usually let you get pretty close. If you tried to get out, they'd probably run away—although some have been known to charge.

The largest enclosure at Safari West is the exclusive domain of a herd of long-horned Watusi cattle—large, intimidating creatures. "These guys can be pretty ornery when they want to be," Mike says. "But in Africa you commonly see large herds of these cattle with a ten- or twelve-year-old boy walking right through them and milking them! And anybody who can milk a Watusi has got my respect."

On the walking tour of the smaller enclosures, you'll see exotic birds and mammals from all over the world—possibly even some female kangaroos with babies, called joeys, in their pouches.

You might also get close to a giraffe on the walking tour. The preserve's several giraffes include two Masai giraffes, native to Kenya. When they get older,

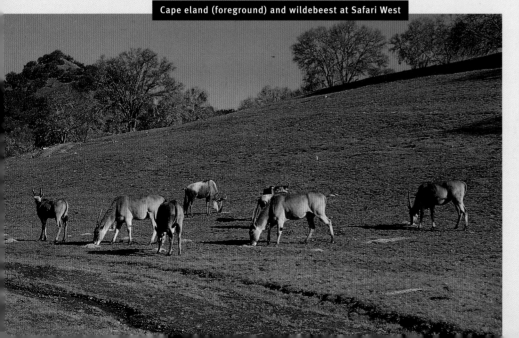

Cape eland (foreground) and wildebeest at Safari West

Masai giraffe at Safari West

Mike hopes to breed them and continue the success Safari West is having with other endangered species, such as the addax, the scimitar-horned oryx, and the bongo. With the increasing loss of wild habitat and threats from poachers, captive breeding programs such as this may offer these animals their best chance for long-term survival. As Mike Farley likes to say, "I just can't imagine an earth without a bongo on it."

Safari West 707-579-2551

NIEBAUM-COPPOLA WINERY, AND TWO UNUSUAL STORES IN YOUNTVILLE

19

A road trip north of San Francisco, along Highway 29 through the Napa Valley, is a journey through exquisite rural beauty and intriguing history, where roots grow deep for both grapevines and families.

Highway 29 will take you past some of the most famous wineries in the world, as well as some of the best restaurants in California. The Napa Valley is known worldwide for its appreciation of the good life, good food, and good wine. This tradition stretches back almost one hundred and fifty years to a time just after the Gold Rush.

Nowhere is Napa Valley history more evident than at Niebaum-Coppola, an estate winery that sits at the end of a long sweeping driveway near Rutherford off Highway 29. "This was Inglenook," says filmmaker Francis Ford Coppola. "And Inglenook is historically one of the most important wineries in America, and therefore in the world."

Francis and his wife, Eléanor, are restoring the Inglenook estate that dates back to 1879. "This was the great lady of the Napa Valley," continues Francis. "And largely the fame of the Napa Valley as a wine growing region is because of Inglenook and Beaulieu Vineyards, and maybe two or three other great institutions."

Gustave Niebaum, a young sea captain from Finland, created this two-thousand-acre wine estate with the fortune he made in Alaska. Niebaum was an innovator. He established winemaking practices that were a century ahead of their time, and the Inglenook ranch was the first in California to have electricity.

Niebaum made wine that was considered by many to be America's best. But economic hardship in the 1960s forced Niebaum's heirs to sell off the Inglenook name and split up the estate. The vineyards were left untended, and developers were scheming to cover the hillsides with sixty homes.

The Coppolas first saw the land in 1974, and they couldn't resist the beauty of Niebaum's property. The next year they bought Niebaum's house and enough acreage to begin making their own wine. "We made wine," recalls Francis, "and it came out good. Basically, grapes know on their own how to make wine. You just have to squish them."

In the years since, the Coppolas' wines have gained international recognition for their high quality. In 1995, Francis and Eleanor purchased the remainder of the Inglenook estate, including a massive

Niebaum-Coppola Winery

ously. "I wasn't nuts about wine when I was a kid," remembers Francis. "We would mix it up with ginger ale or lemon soda and make it really good. And today, my daughter mixes it with Orangina!"

After your visit to the Coppolas, consider stopping by two curious places nearby. Both are unusual stores—one a factory full of lights, the other a store full of magazines—that will keep you busy for a while.

The Wood-U-Love store in Yountville is home to Merle Harris's extensive collection of *Life* magazines. He has spent more than a decade putting together his collection. "We have every issue that *Life* ever published," says Merle. "They're great birthday gift items. You can get them pretty close to your birthday because they came out once a week. We have about fifteen thousand to twenty thousand of them in our warehouse now," claims Merle, "probably one of the largest collections in the United States." From presidents to movie stars to life-altering events, seven decades of history and life are captured on these pages and in this store.

About twenty minutes north of Yountville on Highway 29 you'll come across the Hurd Beeswax candle factory. They've been making and selling wax creations since 1954. "There really is nothing else quite like this because this is pure bees-

stone chateau. They have set out to create an inviting atmosphere for visitors. It's also one they enjoy themselves.

The grounds of the chateau are reminiscent of a French park. Cafe tables invite leisurely conversations over glasses of wine. Inside the chateau, a grand staircase handcrafted from exotic woods leads to a banquet hall that's available for private gatherings. A museum chronicles the history of winemaking at the estate and Coppola's own history in filmmaking.

The tasting room and store reflect the Coppolas' appreciation of the good life and a keen sense for marketing. Visitors are enticed by specialty foods, cook-

books, movie memorabilia, daughter Sofia's clothing line, and, of course, signature wines on which the Coppolas give top billing to Captain Niebaum.

"We have planted the seed for this estate to go on," says Francis. "We hope that we've taken the steps to enable it to never be broken up again, to never have structures on that hill. Hopefully this place will be like a park that belongs to the people."

In the meantime, it's a place that the Coppolas call home, where the moviemaker and his family are learning to appreciate wine, but not take it too seri-

wax, it's not paraffin, which is what most candles are made out of," says Marysue Frediani, one of the owners. "They're all handmade, unique designs that were created by the Hurds back in 1954."

Workers are busy in the factory and in the hive. "There's a wonderful demonstration beehive, which is always buzzing," says Marysue. "There are baby bees that are hatching out and, yes, there is a queen in there."

The Napa Valley can get crowded on weekends. It's best to come on weekdays if you can. But whenever you come, no matter the season, the valley is beautiful. Take time to enjoy Napa's many wineries and restaurants, explore its public parklands and historic sites, and walk the streets of its quaint small towns, such as St. Helena and Calistoga. Or see the whole valley at once in a slow and sensuous early morning float in a hot air balloon. Give yourself the time to stay in one of the many exquisite and romantic inns. In Napa Valley the wine requires time, and so do we.

Niebaum-Coppola Winery 707-968-1100
Wood-U-Love 800-952-2243
Hurd Beeswax Candles
    800-977-7211/707-963-7211
Napa Valley Balloons 800-253-2224
Calistoga Balloon Adventures
    800-400-0162

The chateau at Niebaum-Coppola Winery

20

JACK LONDON STATE PARK AND GLEN ELLEN:
Sonoma Valley's Quiet Sanctuaries

In the early years of the twentieth century, Jack London was one of the most popular, successful, and famous writers alive. Strikingly handsome and full of laughter, he was an early celebrity. He was also a daring adventurer who wrote numerous books, including *White Fang, Call of the Wild,* and *The Sea Wolf.* In his life, he took the roles of sailor, laborer, war correspondent, lecturer, oyster pirate, hobo, gold prospector, socialist, and finally—innovative farmer.

Jack London was also a native son of the Bay Area. He was born in San Francisco and grew up in Oakland. He discovered his love of words at the Oakland Public Library, and his love of sailing on the waters of San Francisco Bay. You can find out all about Jack London on a beautiful backroads trip to Sonoma County and what London called "The Valley of the Moon."

An hour and a half north of his hometown of Oakland is the village of Glen Ellen, just off Highway 12. London visited in 1903 when he was becoming weary of

The remains of Wolf House, Jack London State Park

Sonoma Valley grapevines

rejection notices from his early days.

While London was developing his ranch he also continued to travel the world as he always had. He built the *Snark* and sailed the South Seas for twenty-seven months between 1906 and 1909 in search of adventure and stories to tell. Over the years London pushed himself to write a thousand words a day and he turned them into fifty-one books and countless short stories and articles.

Although he was tight for money after purchasing the Beauty Ranch, London eventually produced enough work to afford the construction of his dream home, a twenty-six-room mansion he called Wolf House. Tragically, the house was destroyed by fire less than a month before he was to move in. According to Matt, when Wolf House burned London lost some of his passion for life. These days, the stone walls and the other ghostly remains of Wolf House stand silently in a deepening forest, a bitter-

cities. He fell in love with the valley and bought a farm he called Beauty Ranch. He lived here with his second wife, Charmian, until his death in 1916.

Today a good portion of Beauty Ranch is Jack London State Historic Park. "The word that comes to mind for Jack London is vitality," says Matt Atkinson, a ranger at the park since 1977. "He was full of life. He came here because he once said he was looking for a place in the country where he could get away from the city. Where he could rest and relax, and where he could get out of nature 'that something we all need.' He found it here."

Visitors will find the same remarkable

beauty that once inspired London. There are ten miles of hiking trails, many available to mountain bikers and horse riders. The trails lead through a variety of environments, from oak woodlands to open grasslands, vineyards, and dense groves of redwoods. One trail leads to a secluded pond where Jack and Charmian enjoyed swimming.

The House of Happy Walls, the home Charmian built after Jack died at the age of forty, is now a museum and the park's visitors center. It houses his desk, fascinating memorabilia, some original manuscripts, and an impressive collection of

"It is so much easier to live placidly and complacently. Of course, to live placidly and complacently is not to live at all. . . ."

JACK LONDON

The Glen Ellen Center

sweet reminder of a remarkable man and his vanished dreams.

Jack London's ashes are at home now on Beauty Ranch, buried beneath a big red boulder that was once part of Wolf House. Despite his achievements there is no monument there to London. That's the way he would have wanted it—very simple. Although he died more than eight decades ago, many still think of him as a thoroughly modern character. In all sorts of ways he had an insatiable curiosity and a relentless energy that would have served him well in our restless times.

To find out even more about Jack London, go to the town of Glen Ellen and visit the Jack London Bookstore. Winnie Kingman has spent more than two decades running the place. "I would say that Jack London was a man's man," says Winnie with a smile, "but the women chased him. You know, I don't know if it would have been beneficial if he had lived any longer. I think he accomplished so much in those forty years, and set such an example, that maybe it was enough. He didn't just exist, he *lived*."

While in Glen Ellen, take some time to walk around. It's an appealing village with a population of about a thousand. It has some pleasant places to eat, to stay, and to taste local wine. Its rich history and magnetic beauty have made Glen Ellen a popular Bay Area getaway since the late 1800s. The Sonoma Valley and

Glen Ellen have long attracted passionately creative people from the early winegrowers to the likes of Jack London. And the region still attracts modern-day Jack Londons—creative people who explore the globe and could live anywhere else, but have an affection for this place.

One creative Sonoma Valley resident is Norton Buffalo, known as the Harmonica King. He earns his keep playing clubs and concerts as well as writing and recording albums. In fact, Norton plays harmonica on the *Bay Area Backroads* theme song.

"I travel all over the world, and this is where I come back to be home," says Norton. "It's common for me to be on the road eight months every year, and you don't know how good it feels to come back to this valley. I understand why Jack London settled here," Norton continues, "he wanted to come back and be somewhere where he could write and be at peace with himself. That place he built on the mountain is just an incredible sanctuary."

The Glen Ellen Center, located downtown, celebrates the valley's farming and winemaking history. In the surrounding hills, that history is still alive today. And even though Glen Ellen has made a few concessions to the modern age, it hasn't changed much since London's day. He would probably still feel right at home mingling with visitors and neighbors at a local tavern and telling tales of his world adventures.

Jack London State Historic Park
  707-938-5216
Sonoma Valley Visitor's Bureau
  707-996-1090
  http://www.sonomavalley.com
Jack London Bookstore 707-996-2888
Glen Ellen Center 707-939-6277

PAPA'S TAVERNA

A road trip to Sonoma can offer a taste of the Greek Isles. Papa's Taverna, a very special Greek restaurant, sits on the banks of the Petaluma River, at a place called Gilardi's Marina. It's north of Highway 37, and south of Petaluma, off Lakeville Road. On Sunday afternoons, between 2:30 and 8:00, Papa's Taverna is the center of the universe for people who love food, music, dance, and the Greek way of life.

"The best thing for me is when I see people smile," says Leo Papageorge, the Taverna's proprietor and patriarch. "You see the grandmothers, you see the little kids—the beginning, and the end. And both of them laughing. That means enjoyment, and love. This is life!"

Papa's is the place to fulfill any Zorba the Greek fantasies you might have. They have what they call Greek lessons at the Taverna: you can easily pick up a few folk dancing steps, and then, fueled by some of the good Greek food Leo serves up, you'll soon be one of a line of fellow dancers, your arms around the shoulders of perfect strangers, legs kicking in time with the music, burning enough calories to justify more food.

"It's not only the Greeks that enjoy coming here," says co-owner Lana Sutton, "it's all the Americans. Everyone else is starting to get into the swing of things. I'm not Greek, but when you work here, you become Greek."

And if being Greek gets a little overwhelming, you can step outside, stroll along the docks, and enjoy the quiet beauty of the Petaluma River.

Papa's Taverna: Dancing lessons are on Sundays from 12:30 to 2:30; open dancing follows from 2:30 until 8:00 P.M. There is also dancing on Friday and Saturday nights. 707-769-8545

TOMALES TO BODEGA:
A Gentle Landscape of Traditions and Laughter

21

One of the most wonderful road trips in the Bay Area leads to the little fishing town of Bodega Bay along the Sonoma County coastline. It is a romantic destination, but getting there is at least half the fun.

The best roads to Bodega Bay are unhurried tracks. They pass through welcoming little towns that love a good laugh; they saunter through rolling hills where traditions are being kept alive from halfway around the world. And they lead to a place where the horsepower is under a saddle, not the hood, and where the scenery is unforgettable.

Bodega Bay is northwest of San Francisco. The fastest route takes about an hour and a half following Highway 101 north to Petaluma and then turning west on East Washington Avenue. Continue on the Petaluma Valley Ford Road, skirting the hamlet of Bloomfield. But if you prefer the slow road, Highway One—twisting through the scenic hills of west Marin County—will take you to the little town of Tomales along the way.

John McCall and Rome Sartori are dairy farmers who have lived here most of their lives. "Now we stop at the stop signs in town," says John with a laugh. "In the old days you just blew your horn and kept on driving because there was nobody else around." But some things may never change in Tomales. They still have no stoplights. "No," continues Rome chuckling, "no stoplights. Not yet. And maybe we'll be getting electricity soon!"

Laughter has lit up the town since its very beginning in 1850. Tomales grew up during the Gold Rush and matured while supplying milk and meat to the booming Bay Area. Milk and meat are still the base of the town's economy.

Dio Choperena is of Basque heritage. He was born and raised in the mountains bordering France and Spain. In the hills near Tomales, Dio continues a tradition—tending sheep the way his ancestors have for generations. "The countryside here is pretty much like the Basque country," states Dio. "The only difference is that Basque country is green all year round."

Out here where the Old World and the Wild West are joined, Dio lives out a fantasy. "When I was seventeen," says Dio, "I had a dream of coming to America and herding sheep. I don't know," he continues with a smile, "I guess I watched too many John Wayne movies or something." Dio first moved to Wyoming, then came to the Tomales area in 1980.

Today his John Wayne dreams have become reality, and he has no plans to move on. Most folks in these parts seem to share Dio's sentiment. "It's really heaven out here, really!" exclaims Rome. "You're an hour from San Francisco, and only five minutes from the ocean. But don't play it up *too* much!" "That's right," injects John with another laugh, feigning concern about hordes of potential visitors. "We have a lot of rattlesnakes around here, right Rome? And the septic system is terrible!"

Highway One pushes on past the farmlands near Tomales—and the local jokers—toward the coast and Bodega Bay. From its earliest days, Bodega Bay has made its living as a fishing port. The town has changed somewhat over the years—tourists now outnumber those who fish—but the heart of Bodega is still the ocean.

Jim Clegg spends a lot of time along the shoreline here studying seals and their marine environment. He's a scientist and the director of the Bodega Marine Lab, just outside of town. "People come here from all over to view the ocean, to play in it, and to learn about it," says Jim.

Bodega Bay

Bodega Bay

adventures—the Chanslor Guest Ranch. There are ponies to ride and barnyard animals to feed, and a trail to the beach that the horses know well. It's great fun for the entire family.

Ranch manager Dodie Wallace often takes guests on rides into Bodega Dunes State Beach. While riding along through a glorious maze of rolling dunes, Dodie enjoys teaching guests about the coastal terrain and its wildlife. "In the late spring and early summer," says Dodie, "we often see osprey resting with their fish, before they carry them back to their young." As you ride along, often into the fog, the sound of the pounding surf grows louder and louder. And then, as if a curtain is lifted, the final grass-covered dune gives way to a sweeping view of the Pacific and a long and sandy beach. It's the perfect location for a slow sunset trot.

Between Tomales and Bodega Bay, good humor flourishes, and so do John Wayne fantasies—both on horseback along the beach and with shepherds in the hills.

"This is a protected marine reserve, a fairly rare commodity along the coast. And it's a very important feature of the region. I don't know whether the seals know that or not, but they certainly spend a lot of time here within the reserve."

The lab, run by the University of California, is used by scientists and students to conduct research on the ocean, the creatures that inhabit it, and the land nearby. The public is welcome during lab hours to tour part of the facility and see scientists at work.

Just minutes away from the lab, you can return to the town of Bodega Bay and relax, seek out fresh seafood to eat, and explore places to stay overnight. Just north of town is another spot not only to sleep, but also to head out on horseback

Bodega Marine Labs 707-875-2211
Bodega Bay Chamber of Commerce
   707-875-3422
Bodega Dunes State Beach
   707-875-3483
Chanslor Guest Ranch 707-875-2721

POINT REYES:
More Than a Seashore

22

Point Reyes is blessed with multiple personalities. You can walk along windswept bluffs at Tomales Point. You can climb through dense forest to emerge on steep ridgelines covered with fragrant chaparral, or lose yourself down miles of vacant beaches. This National Seashore and its adjacent lands are also steeped in human history.

Point Reyes National Seashore, with its impressive wildlands, is one of the greatest outdoor destinations in the Bay Area. It's also one of the closest natural areas—less than forty miles from downtown San Francisco on Highway One.

The varied personalities of Point Reyes are easy to experience, even indoors, where diversity and history are on display at the Bear Valley Visitor Center. The center is a lovely spot, well worth a stop. Inside the large barnlike building you'll find excellent displays, a small bookstore, and friendly staff ready to answer questions.

Just a few hundred yards from the visitors center, a couple of other fascinating places interpret the human and natural histories of Point Reyes. Kule Loklo, just a short walk away, is a re-creation of a native Miwok village, depicting a culture whose roots in Point Reyes stretch back thousands of years.

"Kids are amazed that people could live in something so simple, yet survive," says ranger Lanny Pinola, talking about a Miwok shelter. Lanny works at Kule Loklo to help dispel myths many people have about the area's original human inhabitants. "Sometimes they talk about Indians in the past tense," comments Lanny, "like we're not alive today. But we are." At Kule Loklo you can learn not only how the area's first residents lived, but also how their descendants carry on their traditions.

It's not only the Native American people and their traditions that are alive at Point Reyes. So is the land itself. Near the visitors center, follow the appropriately named Earthquake Trail to the San Andreas fault.

The famous fault comes right up the middle of the Peninsula, near towns such as Saratoga and Woodside, then goes out to sea just south of San Francisco. It ventures back inland at Bolinas Lagoon—in West Marin—then parallels Highway One and runs through Point Reyes alongside the visitors center.

On April 18, 1906, the fault ruptured. San Franciscans were rudely awakened by a nearly 8.3 magnitude earthquake, the

Point Reyes National Seashore

worst disaster in California history. Thousands of people were killed, and twenty-eight thousand buildings were destroyed by the tremor and the fires it started.

The force of the 1906 quake has been estimated to be twelve thousand times more powerful than the atomic bomb dropped on Hiroshima. It ripped the land along the San Andreas fault like a giant mole racing northward. Fortunately, the earthquake left no casualties in the rural landscape—only some very tall tales. Earthquake expert Bruce Bolt explains what happened at Point Reyes that day. "In a matter of seconds the earth along the fault was offset by some sixteen feet," says Bruce, pointing to the reconstructed fence exhibit along the trail. The fence, oriented perpendicular to the fault, is now two distinct fences, separated by exactly sixteen feet of open space.

"There's a story of a cow," Bruce continues, "which fell into a big crevasse that opened along the fault during the earthquake. But by the time someone named Dr. Gilbert arrived, there was only the tail of the cow sticking out of the ground. Years afterward, I had some correspondence with people who were the children of those who were living at the time. Turns out that the cow had died a day before and the farmer just put it into a hole in the ground. So it was a tale of a tail."

The San Andreas fault is like a big geology book, wide open for people to look at. You can walk along Sir Francis Drake Boulevard, west of Olema, and imagine what it looked like in 1906 when the earthquake offset the road eighteen feet. You can ride your bike right on the fault, probably without even realizing it. Or you can just enjoy the scenery and remember that we owe all of this to forces of nature that sometimes endanger us.

The forces that created Point Reyes National Seashore may be dangerous, but today the peninsula is protecting ways of life. There are woodpeckers hoarding acorns; working ranches and dairy farms that have been in operation since the mid-1800s; and elephant seals that have returned from the brink of extinction and established a new colony.

A trail near the Chimney Rock parking lot leads to a great view of elephant seals and their wintering spot along Drake's Bay. The seals have found shelter behind the last pinnacle of land out here—Point Reyes itself, where a historic beacon stands, more than a hundred years old.

The lighthouse at Point Reyes is one

Tule elk

of the most scenic spots along the entire California coast. It can also be one of the foggiest. Charles Zetterquist knows this because his father was the lighthouse keeper at Point Reyes from 1930 until 1951. "One of the ways they would tell if it was time to start the foghorn," recalls Charles, "is that they'd hear a ship blowing their whistle. They'd get out and look. If you couldn't see the ship, you'd better start the old foghorn."

When it wasn't foggy, Charles and his family had one of the best views in the Bay Area. Their house was perched 433 steps above the lighthouse. Today the lighthouse is automated and the house is long gone. Its foundation supports visitors who flock here in the winter, scanning the sea for whales.

People also come to Point Reyes to see tule elk. These majestic elk are part of an amazing success story. They were once hunted so extensively that they nearly became extinct. One hundred years ago, only a handful of tule elk remained. But with protection and restoration of their natural habitat—and time—they made a comeback. Today, there are more than five thousand in California, and more than five hundred live in Point Reyes.

The elk herds roam in the Tomales Point area of Point Reyes. You can park your car at Pierce Point Ranch and head out on foot. Most of the time you'll see

Abbotts Lagoon

the elk without any problem. Sometimes they even hang out next to the parking lot. But remember, they're wild animals and could charge if frightened. So enjoy them from a little distance and marvel at how they and the sweeping landscape so beautifully complement each other.

Another welcome aspect of the Point Reyes area is that you can spend all day outdoors exploring history and nature, and then retreat indoors and enjoy terrific food and great places to stay. Olema, Point Reyes Station, and Inverness Park all have excellent restaurants and inns. Camping

is another good option in the vicinity.

Point Reyes can be a wonderful day trip or a weekend outing for people anywhere in the Bay Area. The region is a complex mosaic of nature and history that feels as if it's a world away. Fortunately for us, it's just down the open road.

Point Reyes National Seashore
415-663-1092
West Marin Chamber of Commerce
415-663-9232

MOUNT TAMALPAIS:
A Backyard Wilderness
with a Railroading Past

The land throughout southern Marin
County appears to sweep upward toward
the impressive summit of Mount Tamalpais. But the truth is, Mount Tamalpais is
not very tall. In fact, at less than three
thousand feet it would barely be a foothill
in the Sierra Nevada. But it has the dignity
and presence of a much grander mountain.

People are drawn to Mount Tamalpais
by its physical beauty and wondrous
views. They also seek out the mountain
so their spirits might soar, and so that
they can connect with nature. Some sit
atop the mountain's peaks and ridgelines
to experience the subtle changes of
season and dramatic changes of weather.

Bill Provines has lived at the foot of
Mount Tam in Mill Valley since the early
1900s. He has warm and vivid memories
about its history most of us have forgotten
or never known—the Mount Tamalpais
and Muir Woods Railway, the "crookedest
railroad in the world." Bill worked on the
engines during his college days at Cal. "I
went to work firing the locomotives on the
12th of July, 1926, and worked every day
during the summer."

Alpine Lake, Marin Municipal Water District

Mount Tamalpais

The railroad began chugging up Mount Tamalpais in 1896, and even though it made its last run in 1930, remnants are still to be found on the mountain and in downtown Mill Valley at The Depot. After rains, it's not uncommon for hikers or mountain bikers to find exposed railroad spikes on the old train route, now a fire road.

These days The Depot is a bookstore and coffee shop, but once upon a time it was a busy little railroad station. It was the town center and starting point for the mountain railroad. People from San Francisco took ferries across the bay to Sausalito, making their way to Mill Valley for the chance to ride the rails to the top of Mount Tam. The train snaked its way up the mountain on its one hour and fifteen minute journey to the summit, costing each passenger $1.50.

The entire route of the mountain railway still exists. Today, folks can follow the Railroad Grade (now a fire road) up toward the summit, where the only remaining structure from that railroading era still stands, the West Point Inn. The Inn was built in the early 1900s as a stopping point where people could catch a stagecoach down to Stinson Beach

Mount Tamalpais hikers

and Bolinas, or eat and spend the night.

Cris Chater grew up in Mill Valley, and her love for Mount Tam led her to make a documentary film about the railroad's history. According to Cris, a tavern with sweeping views of the Bay Area once graced the top of Mount Tamalpais. "West Point Inn," says Cris, "was more of a picnic spot—very rustic—and the tavern at East Peak was the fancy place where people waltzed and had a sit-down dinner." For some, dancing at the summit was the highlight of the trip. For others, like Bill, it was the ride back down in the gravity cars. "It was the world's longest rollercoaster," recalls Bill. "You could go seven and a half miles from the top of the mountain down to Muir Woods, and it was just on gravity." The gravities, as the open-air cars were called, made the return trip down the mountain at a steady twelve miles per hour, each car carrying thirty passengers on an exhilarating ride. A brakeman in the rear kept each car from picking up too much speed.

The gravity cars, and the entire railroad, began to lose business in the late 1920s. The construction of the Panoramic Highway in 1928 allowed motorists to drive their cars to Mount Tamalpais's summit and out to the beach. The railroad closed in 1930. Nowadays, Mount Tam's scenic roadways are often used to film car commercials. The methods of transportation

> "The last ascent was very steep. We climbed up the rocks, and just as we reached the highest crag the fog began to clear away. Then came glimpses of the beautiful landscape through the fog. It was most grand, more like some views in the Alps than anything I have seen before—those glimpses of the landscape beneath through foggy curtains. But now the fog and clouds rolled away and we had a glorious view indeed—the ocean on the west, the bay around, the green hills beneath with lovely valleys between them."
>
> WILLIAM H. BREWER,
> March 28, 1862,
> *Up and Down California*

may have changed, but the views haven't.

All of Mount Tamalpais's natural beauty has been preserved for the public by a combination of Mount Tamalpais State Park, Muir Woods National Monument, and the Marin Municipal Water District.

"Look how close it is to the city," says ranger Neil Fogarty from a ridgeline on Tam. Neil works for the Marin Municipal Water District, an agency that manages twenty thousand acres of the mountain to provide water for thousands of homes and businesses in Marin County. Seven dams were built on the mountain's northern slopes between 1873 and 1979 to collect water from the creeks and to catch rain from storms passing over Mount Tamalpais's Bolinas Ridge. "People have a wonderful opportunity to come out here and enjoy Mount Tamalpais," Neil continues, "to enjoy the redwood trees and the lakes." Lush, fern-lined trails take hikers and bikers along cascading creeks, and picturesque lakes. Dogs on leashes are welcome in the watershed area, too.

It's possible to explore the trails and fire roads of Mount Tamalpais for hours and see only a few people. Then you round a corner and suddenly find yourself looking down on a megalopolis of more than six million people. It's a reminder that Mount Tamalpais is—and has been for a very long time—a world apart in the midst of our daily lives.

Mount Tamalpais State Park
　415-388-2070
Cris Chater's film, *Steaming Up Tamalpais*
　415-383-6138
Marin Municipal Water District
　415-924-4600

24 THE MARIN HEADLANDS: A Quick Escape

One of the best things about living in the Bay Area is that within a matter of minutes you can escape the hustle and bustle of the city and disappear into nature's wonderland. One of the best escape options doubles as one of the most dramatic urban landscapes in the world—the Marin Headlands.

These magnificent rolling hills on the northern shore of the Golden Gate can be magical. They are also a good place to elude the world of work, commutes, and the routine hassles that can make life a chore. The headlands—which are part of the Golden Gate National Recreation Area—make you feel a thousand miles away and yet you can still see San Francisco.

At first the headlands may seem crowded as you take Conzelman Road off Highway 101 at the north end of the Golden Gate Bridge. After all, this is where thousands of tourists come to take pictures of San Francisco's skyline. Who can blame them? A lot of us who live here bring visitors out to admire the unparalleled views.

But when most people get to the top

Golden Gate Bridge from the Marin Headlands

of Conzelman Road, they turn the car around and head back to the city. If you keep going instead, you'll find a great get-away—a one-hour vacation or an all-day adventure.

The road takes a headfirst plunge down the headlands, but don't worry, it's one-way, and the speed limit is fifteen miles an hour. Conzelman Road winds along some spectacular coastline. You'll pass historic military gun batteries built to protect the bay, a lighthouse built on Point Bonita in 1855, and a Nike missile base from Cold War days. In the spring wildflowers are everywhere, and each autumn thousands of hawks and monarch butterflies migrate south across the land-scape.

Soon you drop into picturesque Rodeo Valley via McCullough Road and continue on Bunker Road. Its lagoon is a haven for waterfowl, and its long beach and strong waves are a haven for surfers. Throughout the headlands there are per-fect places to stop and read a book, take a rest, or explore. Fire roads, ideal for mountain biking, climb the open hills. Some fifty miles of hiking trails meander through the valleys and over the ridges, and dogs are allowed here as long as they are leashed.

For something really special, try sight-seeing on horseback. Linda Rubio runs the Miwok Livery Stables in the Tennes-

Marin Headlands Visitors Center

see Valley and offers guided trail rides through the headlands. "I just love the fact that I can bring people up here on horseback and look down on San Fran-cisco. I can see the Pyramid Building in the Financial District, and then I like to say 'Ha, ha. I'm up here, and I'm having a good time.'" She continues, "And at the same time you might see a bobcat, some deer, and much more. It's pretty amazing! Being out here also helps you slow down and be closer to nature. You know, horses only know 'yes' or 'no.' Horses don't say,

'I'll think about it,' 'I need to call my attor-ney,' or 'I need to talk to my therapist.'"

For those who wish to stay overnight for some weekend camping, park ranger John Martini has a tip on a secluded spot with a perfect view of the Golden Gate: Kirby Cove. This small inlet and beach is one mile down a fire road from Conzelman Road. It's open to hikers and bicyclists, and it has four campsites, all in very high demand on weekends but often available on weeknights.

"A lot of campers who come down here," says John with a smile, "when the fog is in, have actually registered com-plaints about the foghorns keeping them awake all night. And they often ask if we can turn them off! But there are only so many things the U.S. government has control over—fog is not one of them."

It can get foggy and cool here, so bundle up—or start your visit by going indoors at the Marin Headlands Visitors Center in Rodeo Valley. Kids get to touch and inspect marine shells, stones, and animals. There is also a reed house you can climb into. It is a replica of a coastal Miwok dwelling.

"The center is a place for all ages," says ranger Gayle Lester, "and the great thing about the kids coming is that they get the adults playing again. This is also a starting point for discovering the park. The park has so many stories—natural history and cultural stories. A lot of different folks have lived here. And there are a lot of different animals and habitats out here. So we want people to get a taste, a chance to get a feeling for what they can discover in the headlands."

Marin Headlands Visitors Center
415-331-1540
Marin Headlands Camping Information
415-331-1540/415-561-4304
Miwok Livery Stables 415-383-8048

The Marin Headlands

ANGEL ISLAND:
San Francisco Bay's Island Getaway

If you live in the Bay Area and you want to run away to an exotic island, you don't have to go very far. Just about one mile from the city of Tiburon, across the blue-green waters of Raccoon Straits, is Angel Island State Park. This one-mile-square island is a gorgeous retreat and a time capsule of California history, anchored just offshore.

Ferry boats from San Francisco, Vallejo, and Tiburon—as well as private boats—all dock at the park's Ayala Cove. Many visitors never venture beyond the cove's small beach and picnic grounds, but they should. Hiking trails crisscross the island. Bicycling is popular, too. If you don't want to haul your bicycle over on the ferry you can rent one at Ayala Cove. And if you don't want to pedal or walk, a new tram service lets everyone experience the island's delightful views while listening to an audio tour.

With a little more effort, you can

Camp Reynolds

explore Angel Island's remarkable coastline; kayak trips around the island begin in the cove. You can join a trip even if you've never kayaked before. Each is professionally guided by Bob Licht and his staff at Sea Trek.

"You can really feel what's going on in the bay," says Bob. "You feel every current, every ripple. And you can get so close to the edge of the island you can really get an intimate feel for it in a way that you never can by land."

Kayaking around Angel Island provides an unusual look at its natural beauty. But when you go back ashore, you can gain an appreciation for the history of the island. The old immigration

Chinese Immigration Memorial, Angel Island

station, known as the Ellis Island of the West, was the entry point for most of the Chinese who came to the United States in the early 1900s. Paul Chow saved the station from demolition in the late 1960s. He takes pride in showing school groups the poetry carved into the walls by those who waited on the island, sometimes for years, to enter the country. "My father was kept here," recalls Paul. "He and the others were locked in their rooms twenty-four hours a day, and they weren't allowed to leave until they went through interrogation."

Angel Island was actually called Fort McDowell for a long time, beginning in about 1900. A military hospital was in

Ayala Cove's Namesake

"The longboat was lowered and I set out in it to find a better anchoring ground for the ship. I was looking over the island that I called Angels' Island, the largest one in this harbor, and making close search for an anchoring place that handily provided water and firewood."

Captain Juan Manuel de Ayala, aboard the *San Carlos*, August 12, 1775. He was the first European to sail into San Francisco Bay.

Island, a group of dedicated citizens fought to turn it into a state park. They succeeded, and the island became a park in 1963. The island's nondenominational chapel, once a safe haven for young soldiers en route to Europe and the Pacific, is now open for weddings.

Whether you are drawn to the island for its history, wildlife, trails, or shoreline, a visit isn't complete without a pilgrimage to the island's summit, Mount Livermore. From its 781-foot crown, you have a 360-degree view of the Bay Area. With the help of clear weather you might even experience what park superintendent Jim Burke calls a Five-Bridge Day. "That's right," states Jim. "On a good day you can see the San Rafael, Golden Gate, Bay, Dumbarton, and San Mateo Bridges."

Angel Island State Park 415-435-1915
Sea Trek 415-488-1060
Angel Island/Tiburon Ferry 415-435-2131

operation through both world wars. During part of the Cold War, the island was an administration center and barracks for a missile base. The missiles have been removed, but not the reminders of the one hundred years Angel Island was occupied by the U.S. military.

The buildings at Camp Reynolds, on the west side of Angel Island, date back to the Civil War. The military buildings on the east side served as one of the country's major processing centers for soldiers fighting in World Wars I and II.

When the military pulled out of Angel

Angel Island from Tiburon

East Bay

From left: Will Geiken on the Tilden Park Miniature Railway (Tour 28)
and Mount Diablo Summit Museum (Tour 29)

BENICIA TO MARE ISLAND:
Art, History, and a Lot More

Magic is being created every weekday in the small town of Benicia bordering the Carquinez Strait. Glowing furnaces and centuries-old techniques yield dynamic creations in the workshops of Nourot, Smyers, and Zellique. These three craftspeople formed the Benicia Glass Studios and collectively they produce some of the world's most exotic and sought-after glass art.

Benicia is an hour's drive northeast of San Francisco off Interstate 80. Take the Interstate 780 turnoff and drive east. Exit at East 5th Street and continue about five blocks toward the Carquinez Strait until you see East H Street and the studios.

The glassblowers' craft hasn't changed much over time: heat glass to about 2,500 degrees, gather it onto a rod or blowpipe, shape, heat again, re-shape. Sounds simple, right? Wrong. Though the process seems routine, the end product is as individual as one's imagination.

The Nourot workshop has had illustrious customers such as the Pope and First Lady Hillary Clinton, who bought several

BENICIA STATE RECREATION AREA

En route to either Benicia or Vallejo and Mare Island, why not visit Benicia State Recreation Area? It's off Interstate 780 on State Park Road. The recreation area spreads over four hundred acres of wild shoreline along the Carquinez Strait. There are several trails you can explore as well as a paved road popular with runners and bikers and a handful of picnic areas. The antics of resident and migratory shorebirds also make a visit worth your while.

Michael Nourot, Benicia Glass Studios

faceted perfume bottles for presentation to the wives of dignitaries. And while Zellique's designs are a tribute to nature's beauty, Steve Smyers' work concentrates on art for the table. "We've had a number of celebrity customers who have bought our glasses—Bette Midler, Richard Dreyfuss, Tina Turner," says Steve. "In fact, Tina Turner bought an entire line of glassware."

On weekdays, the artisans are here blowing glass right behind the showrooms. The salesrooms are open Monday through Saturday. You can walk in and get an up-close look at the fascinating and beautiful process.

The town of Benicia is full of surprises, both artistic and otherwise. It was California's first incorporated city, and it was California's state capital for a brief period a few years after the Gold Rush. The old capitol building is now a state park and open for visitors. Benicia was also home to a huge federal arsenal. One of the large buildings erected in the 1850s as a military warehouse, just a few blocks from the Benicia Glass Studios, is called the Camel Barn Museum today. The Barn serves as a repository of the town's rich past and is operated by the Benicia Historical Museum and Cultural Foundation.

For another glimpse into the region's past, consider leaving Benicia on Interstate 780 and moving westward. You'll pass under Interstate 80 and continue through the town of Vallejo to historic Mare Island. Tours of the island are available through the Mare Island Historic Park Foundation.

Mare Island was the first naval base on the West Coast. It was founded by David G. Farragut. His work at Mare Island, and later capturing New Orleans during the Civil War, led to his promotion as the first Admiral of the U.S. Navy. The shipyard was in operation from 1854 until 1996. Exactly 513 ships were built here, from the side-wheeling *Saginaw*,

Tiffany stained-glass windows, St. Peter's Chapel

to the USS *Drum,* a nuclear-powered submarine.

Ken Zadwick, founder of the Mare Island Historic Park Foundation, is trying to preserve hundreds of landmarks on the island. "For example," says Ken, "one of the dry docks on the island dates to the 1870s. It was built from hand-cut stone brought down from the Sierra. The other dry docks are cement, so this is unusual." There are also more than two thousand artifacts in storage, which the foundation hopes to display one day in a museum.

Mare Island has military history and a whole lot more. The island's Alden Park displays cannons, a Polaris missile, and even a World War I German suicide submarine. But it's also ringed by trees brought in from all over the world. And the island's St. Peter's Chapel has the largest collection of Tiffany stained-glass windows west of the Mississippi. Thanks to the foundation's efforts, it's now open for civilian weddings.

Benicia Glass Studios 707-745-5710
Camel Barn Museum 707-745-5435
Mare Island Historic Park Foundation
    707-557-1538
    http://www.willardsworld.com/html/
    mihp.html

Mare Island's hand-cut granite dry dock

EAST BROTHER LIGHT STATION:
San Francisco Bay's Unique Bed-and-Breakfast

Lamp house at East Brother Light Station

On the backroads, you can travel far and wide to find unique and sometimes romantic places. But often, you don't have to travel anywhere. For example, you can find a historic light station and a romantic bed-and-breakfast inn on a little island in San Francisco Bay.

It's called East Brother Light Station, and it's been a beacon on the bay since 1873. East Brother stands guard just a few miles north of the Richmond–San Rafael Bridge.

John Barnett and his wife Lore were the innkeepers at East Brother when *Bay Area Backroads* stopped by. "Basically, the United States' castles are their light stations," said John with a laugh. "This light station was built because there wasn't much light in the area in the 1870s and the ships traveling up to Vallejo and Sacramento needed a safe shipping channel. You could see for a long distance in all directions from here."

You may have a pretty romantic notion of light stations, but in the old days, being a light station keeper was hard work. The

light needed constant maintenance, and bringing supplies onto the island was a major ordeal. Today, getting to and from East Brother is quite a bit easier, as long as you can find Western Drive, the road to the San Pablo Yacht Harbor in Richmond. Western Drive is the last turnoff from Interstate 580, heading west, just before the Richmond–San Rafael Bridge toll plaza.

Western Drive is rich with history. The shoreline here was home to Chinese shrimp fishermen around the turn of the century, and up to one hundred sardine boats docked here during the 1940s. The imposing building on the shoreline that you pass—the one that looks like a medieval fortress—was built in the early 1900s as a winery known as Winehaven. It was once thought to be the largest winery

in the world. Prohibition caused its demise in the 1920s, and now the site is a Navy fuel depot.

Just when you're beginning to wonder if you're on the right road, the well-hidden San Pablo Yacht Harbor comes into view. While you're waiting for the motorboat to pick you up and take you to the light station, you may want to take a walk and check out the community garden at the end of the harbor.

The boat ride is quick. Along the way, you'll glimpse another surprising piece of the area's past—the burned-out remains of the West Coast's last whaling station. You can see it on the tip of Point San Pablo; local whalers hauled in gray whales and other species here until 1971, when the business was shut down by federal order after the United States banned commercial whaling.

East Brother Light Station

As you approach the light station, you'll be able to see why it's called East Brother. The rock next to it is West Brother Island. East Brother looked like its sibling until its top was blasted off to make way for the light station.

What makes the island's inn unique is the setting. You can sit and watch big ships and little seals cruise by, or gaze at the reposing birds or the rushing tide below the dock. There's a sense of intimacy here and a feeling of remoteness, even though it's just a short distance to the mainland.

It may be romantic, but it's also expensive. Rooms cost $325 a night for couples and $235 a night for singles, including breakfast and a gourmet dinner. But there's a way to enjoy the island for much less. You can come out for the day for about $10, which buys you transportation and a short tour. You can also have a picnic outside on the island.

Whether you come for the day or stay overnight, you may be treated to a sound heard only from old-time light stations—a real foghorn. It's not really used anymore, but when the innkeepers set it off for visitors, you can hear it ring across San Pablo Bay. It even seems to bounce back off Mount Tamalpais!

After its practical functions became automated, the light station itself was nearly torn down in the early 1970s. Fortunately, a group of citizens came up with the bed-and-breakfast idea to save it. Money generated by the inn is used to restore and maintain the light station. With the help of numerous dedicated volunteers and satisfied visitors, East Brother Light Station has found a new role that should sustain it for decades to come.

East Brother Light Station 510-233-2385

WINEHAVEN

Between 1908 and 1919 Winehaven flourished along the Richmond shoreline. The California Wine Association built the facility because it was close to rail service and shipping lanes. Winehaven produced an impressive variety of wines from grapes grown as far north as Yolo County and as far south as San Bernardino County. Its annual production averaged a whopping twelve million gallons of wine—every month 500,000 gallons were shipped around the world (some three hundred barrels of wine were sent to San Francisco daily!). The story goes that when authorities drained nearly a quarter million gallons of wine into the bay when Prohibition began, local fishermen scooped "marinated" fish off the bay for days.

THE EAST BAY'S STRING OF PARKLAND PEARLS:
From Tilden to Ardenwood

We often travel thousands of miles to escape the daily grind—to find a peaceful spot to get away from it all. But there are places to do that right in your own backyard. In fact, you could easily spend a whole vacation just exploring the East Bay Regional Park District, and you'd still barely scratch the surface.

Some may not realize it, but the East Bay has the most far-reaching network of parks in the Bay Area. Fifty-three parks make up the system, stretching from the bay shoreline about forty miles eastward to the edge of the Delta, from the Sunol-Ohlone Wilderness in the south to Point Pinole in the north, from the volcanic mountains of the Sibley Preserve above Berkeley to Coyote Hills, home of the last major freshwater marsh in Alameda County, to historic Ardenwood—a working turn-of-the-century farm near Fremont. Once you begin to get to know some of these jewels, you'll be amazed at the variety of things you can do and discover.

Tilden Park is a perfect example. Nestled in the Berkeley hills, Tilden is probably the best-known park in the East Bay. Even in this one place, there's a tremendous amount of diversity, both natural and recreational. Besides the miles of hiking trails and the spectacular views of the Bay Area, Tilden Park has a wonderful botanic garden featuring plants from around California. There is Tilden's Little Farm where children line up to feed and pet the animals, a golf course for bigger kids, a merry-go-round, and not one but two different kinds of miniature trains.

Local writer and publisher Malcolm Margolin walked up to Tilden Park the very first day he came to Berkeley in 1968. "I remember sitting there with my friend," recalls Malcolm, "and we looked over the whole bay: Mount Tamalpais, the Marin Headlands, and San Francisco. And then I looked around at Tilden and began hiking. There were all of these plants and trees and flowers, and a deer came out of the

87

brush. And I said to myself, 'my God, I've reached Paradise.' This is it!"

Malcolm wrote a book about the whole East Bay park system, called *The East Bay Out*. He found that the history behind some of the district's parks is quite surprising. Point Pinole, for example, is now three and a half miles of splendid shoreline in north Richmond. But for about a hundred years, gunpowder, dynamite, and eventually nitroglycerine were manufactured there. To find this park exit Interstate 80 at Hilltop Drive and continue to San Pablo Avenue, turn right and continue until Atlas Road. Turn left on Atlas, which becomes Giant Highway, and continue for several miles until you see the park's entrance sign.

Lake Chabot is a peaceful haven between Oakland, Castro Valley, and San Leandro. It was built in 1874 by hydraulic engineer Anthony Chabot. He scoured thousands of tons of dirt off the surrounding hills by aiming huge hoses at them. To pack down the dirt Chabot had herds of wild horses run back and forth across the area. From this strange and difficult beginning, we now have a beautiful lake and park. To find this park exit Interstate 580 in San Leandro onto Fairmont Avenue, moving toward the hills. Continue until Lake Chabot Road and the park's entrance.

"For some people," says Malcolm, "these parks become places of sanity. They become places where they go to restore themselves." Regional park ranger Kevin Fox knows exactly what Malcolm means. "I jump on Highway 880 every day," admits Kevin, "then I spend thirty to forty minutes fighting my way through the traffic. It's hectic. And then you arrive at a park and you feel like you're a million miles away from it all."

Sunol Regional Wilderness—at the southern edge of the district—is one of the largest of the East Bay regional parks, and a good choice for those wishing to *really* get away on miles and miles of challenging trails. But there's also a less strenuous way to experience the hills of Sunol. You can rent horses by the hour or even for overnight trips at the Sunol Pack Station. (In fact, you can ride horses in most of the district's parks.) To find Sunol, exit Interstate 680 onto Calaveras Road and drive south. There are access points along both Welch Creek and Geary roads, both off Calaveras.

One of the district's most unique parks is Ardenwood Historic Farm. Even if you're not familiar with the East Bay, Ardenwood is easy to find—it's just off the intersection

Blacksmith Phil Lawrence at Ardenwood Historic Farm

Botanic garden at Tilden Regional Park

of Interstate 880 and Highway 84 on the Fremont-Newark border. You can see the highways from the farm—a stark contrast between the frenetic pace of today's world and the more relaxed atmosphere of a bygone era.

"Ardenwood is meant to show people what life was like in this part of the Bay Area at the turn of the century," says Ira Bletz, Ardenwood's supervising naturalist. "So what we've done is re-create a turn-of-the-century farm, complete with crops, farm animals, and wagons."

Ardenwood is a great place to take the kids, and the farm operates almost exclusively with technology that was available to farmers in the 1890s. It's a working farm; visitors are encouraged to help with planting, harvesting, and other chores.

"Often we look back at history," reflects Ira, "and it's a very romanticized view. We might look back and think, 'Oh, isn't that quaint the way they once did things.' But really, they were doing it as well as they could with the tools and the equipment they had available. It's hard work being a farmer. There are so many things beyond your control. The weather, pests, timing your harvest properly. I have a lot of respect now for farmers after working here."

You'll probably gain a lot of respect for blacksmiths too after watching one such as Jean Meneley in action. "This skill gives you an appreciation for your ancestors," says Jean. "When you realize that every nail that went into building their house had to be hand-forged! When some people moved, they used to burn the building just to collect the nails and hinges. You didn't just run down to the local hardware store and get what you wanted."

"One of the things I like best about Ardenwood," adds Ira, "is that it's a place you can visit over and over again. It's always changing because everything we do here is tied to the seasons. If you come out in the spring and help us plant corn, you can come back in October and help harvest the same crop. Our program is tied to nature, tied to the seasons, and so every visit is a little bit different."

It's hard to visit Ardenwood without learning a great deal about life on a turn-of-the-century farm, and you're likely to

Will Geiken on the Tilden Park Miniature Railway

have a heck of a lot of fun while you're at it. You might have to work hard during your visit making ice cream the old-fashioned way, and then work again eating it. You'll also be able to forget about the pressures of the outside world for a while—at least until you leave the farm's gate and return to the highways.

Whether your interest is in little trains,

canoes, swimming, picnicking, horseback riding, or meandering trails through nearby wilderness areas, the East Bay's treasure trove of parks is truly rich.

East Bay Regional Park District
510-562-PARK

MOUNT DIABLO: 29
Plants, Animals, and Surrounding Peace

Mount Diablo has some of the best views in the Bay Area. You can see more landmass from Diablo's 3,849-foot summit than from any other place on earth, except for Africa's nineteen thousand-foot Mount Kilamanjaro. To the east you can even see *into* Yosemite Valley on a clear day, and to the north Lassen Peak and Mount Shasta are sometimes visible.

Mount Diablo itself is every bit as spectacular as the views it affords. Being there is a relaxing escape year-round: each season brings a different mood and a new beauty to the mountain. In spring, the hills burst with lush, vibrant colors which mellow slowly to suede brown in summer and fall. Winter's unpredictable storms swell the mountain's waterways and, every so often, dust its peaks with snow, temporarily turning Mount Diablo into a winter wonderland. It's an impressive piece of wildness only thirty miles east of San Francisco, looming above the populous cities of Danville, Walnut Creek, Concord, and Clayton.

There are many ways to enjoy Mount Diablo. The bird-watching is great, the wildflowers are spectacular, and there are more than a dozen excellent hiking trails.

Mount Diablo from the foothills

You can also cruise on your mountain bike, or ride your horse, along miles of fire roads and trails.

Some people explore the mountain with camera in hand. Stephen Joseph is a photographer who makes his living capturing images of Mount Diablo. It's a passion he has pursued for years with the help of a one hundred-year-old camera—a timeless camera for a timeless place.

Stephen photographs the mountain year-round, in all kinds of weather. "For some of my shots," he explains, "I might sit in the same place for four or five hours. While I'm there, a coyote might walk by, and all the birds start to come in

Alexander Lindsay Jr. Museum

real close. I think that sitting and looking can be a very important thing to do, especially up here."

If all you want to do is go for a nice drive through some unforgettable scenery, that's fine too. If you drive to the top of the mountain you'll get an extensive view of the Bay Area. You'll also be able to visit the Mount Diablo Summit Museum, operated by the volunteer-run Mount Diablo Interpretive Association. Inside you'll find dioramas of the mountain's ecology, human history, and geology. Another surprise inside the museum is the mountain's summit itself; the museum is literally built on the tip-top of the peak; a cutaway in the museum's floor lets you kneel down and touch it!

Some people come to the mountain with a multitude of tools in their hands, but a single goal in mind. They come to lend a helping hand to an old friend in need; they are volunteers at Mount Diablo State Park. These people join forces to create new campsites, repair public buildings, and clear trails. And they have a good time doing it.

For people who visit Mount Diablo for the very first time—and for those who know the mountain intimately—the remarks of photographer Stephen Joseph ring true. "This place feels like home," says Stephen. "And I'm very interested in preserving it. I'd like my kids, and their

WALNUT CREEK'S NATURAL SCIENCES MUSEUM

Many of the animals and habitats you might come across on Mount Diablo are on display at the nearby Alexander Lindsay Jr. Museum (510-935-1978)—an interpretive museum and wildlife rehabilitation facility in Walnut Creek on Buena Vista Avenue. The museum has a petting zone where kids can interact with some creatures, and the wildlife rehabilitation program nurses injured animals back to health. Those that recover are returned to the wild; others with more serious injuries remain at the museum and help visitors understand their nonhuman neighbors.

kids, to see it. Especially as the Bay Area becomes more developed, we'll need places like Mount Diablo for our sanity."

Mount Diablo State Park 510-837-2525
Mount Diablo Interpretive Association
510-927-7222

The U.C. Berkeley Campanile

THE UNIVERSITY OF CALIFORNIA, BERKELEY:
A Lot More Than Classes and Homework

The Bay Area is blessed with many fine colleges and universities. One half of a historic cross-bay collegiate rivalry is U.C. Berkeley. Even if you're not an alumnus— and regardless of whether you keep abreast of the Big Game with Stanford— the Berkeley campus is packed with things to do and places to go. Also, its setting—the undulating East Bay hills— can't be beat. Just turn off of Interstate 880 at University Avenue and head toward the hills. You'll drive right onto the Cal campus (make sure to ask for a map at one of the entrance stations).

Where else can you come face to face with a full-sized Tyrannosaurus rex or marvel at some thirteen thousand beautiful and exotic plants? If you seek out the Museum of Paleontology on campus you can find T. rex . . . just don't turn your back on him. Right next door in the Herbarium you can see prickly phlox that was collected in the Sierra Nevada more than a hundred years ago by famed naturalist John Muir; you can also view the world's largest seed, called the double coconut.

Altogether, the Berkeley campus has five museums of natural history and science. One of the more popular spots is the Lawrence Hall of Science, above the campus overlooking the bay. Thousands of schoolkids—and quite a few adults—have been learning about science and having fun here for years. In addition to its permanent exhibits and its wildly popular hands-on attractions, the Hall hosts exciting traveling exhibits.

Cal has other museums, too, including one of the world's largest university art museums and the Phoebe Apperson Hearst Museum of Anthropology. "This museum is one of the best anthropology collections in the country," says museum director Rosemary Joyce. "We generally try to rotate exhibitions in our space because we have four million items in the collection and only six thousand square feet of space. We estimate it would take three hundred years to move everything in and out."

One exhibit that doesn't change is devoted to Ishi, the last known member of the Yahi tribe of Northern California.

Lawrence Hall of Science

Native Californians have long been a major focus of the Hearst Museum. According to Rosemary, many people from different California tribes come here to view the collections to understand more about their own culture.

If you tire of being indoors and need to get a broader perspective on the campus and the Bay Area, try a ride up the Campanile. For fifty cents you can ride the elevator to the top of the 307-foot spire and gaze out over the campus, Berkeley, and the bay beyond. Inside the Campanile, one of the largest collections of ice-age animal bones resides. Mastodon and saber-toothed cat remains inhabit the tower and can be seen on special tours.

If you're inside the Campanile at noon on weekdays, you can see and hear carillon music—a set of bells and a keyboard, housed in the structure—being played up close. It's a wonderful experience, but the bells' sound is pretty loud. Outside, the music is softer and the perfect compliment to a lush and lovely campus.

Moving back indoors, you can study some amazing treasures in a remarkable library. Cal's Bancroft Library is home to an impressive amount of material, and not just books; it even impresses the person in charge of it, Dr. Charles Faulhaber. "The thing that astonishes me," laughs Charles, "is that almost every day someone will mention something they're

T. rex skeleton at the Museum of Paleontology

looking for in here, and my reaction is, 'You mean, we have that, too?'"

Although the majority of the library's holdings are behind closed doors and reserved for researchers, you can find constantly changing exhibits in the front lobby. For example, you might be able to glimpse some of Mark Twain's original writings. According to Charles, the Bancroft has roughly twelve thousand letters written by Mark Twain.

"We also have one of the half dozen Aztec manuscripts in the world," adds Charles. "It's a scroll twenty-one feet long. And we have one of the first two nuggets that was discovered at Sutter's Mill on January 24, 1848, that started the Gold Rush."

Whether gold nuggets, heights, history, big teeth, or botany intrigue you, the Cal campus is a great place to visit—no matter which side of the Big Game rivalry you come down on.

University of California, Berkeley Visitor Information Center 510-642-5215

The First and Last Chance Saloon

OAKLAND BY FOOT, WITH A FEW SURPRISES THROWN IN

Down at the water's edge in Oakland, at the foot of Broadway, is where the city began back in 1852 when a wharf was built to ship lumber and supplies during the Gold Rush. Oakland soon began to grow, but always in the shadow of its colorful and charismatic neighbor, San Francisco. Although Oakland has often been overlooked, it shouldn't be. This town is packed with surprises.

Don Tyler is a strong partisan of the East Bay, or, as he puts it, the "Continental" side of the bay. He teaches high school in Oakland and volunteers as a guide on walking tours of Old Oakland. What Don likes about Oakland is its diversity. "We have something of everything in terms of people, architecture, and neighborhoods."

Oakland's rich variety goes back to its early days. It was this atmosphere that spawned the creativity of such famous residents as Jack London, Bret Harte, and Isadora Duncan.

Writer Gertrude Stein also grew up in Oakland. Her famous quote, "There is no

The USS _Potomac_

they built a duplicate cabin and then disassembled both of them. Each side got half of the original logs and each got some of the new logs."

Next to the log cabin, the First and Last Chance Saloon, once frequented by Jack London, is still an active watering hole. It first opened in 1883. Carol Brookman is only the second owner of this venerable establishment. "If you got too drunk in here way back when," says Carol with a laugh, "you were dropped off into a boat down below. This place was on stilts over a muddy area. And then the next thing you knew, you were on your way to China!"

Not too far down the waterfront from the old saloon—just a casual ten-minute walk—is a piece of presidential history, the USS _Potomac_, President Franklin Roosevelt's yacht. Though FDR only visited the Bay Area once, his ship is now permanently berthed in Oakland—and his legacy is all around the Bay Area. Federal funds given during and after the Depression helped fund the Bay Bridge, Treasure Island, dozens of public schools, hundreds of public buildings, murals in Coit Tower and countless other pieces of public art, and much more.

President Roosevelt spent many delightful hours on the decks of the _Potomac_, cruising the Potomac River near Washington. The ship provided a welcome escape from the enormous pressures of

there there," haunted the city for decades. "What she was referring to was that, when she came back to Oakland after 30 years," says Don, "her house was no longer here, her school was gone, her favorite park was gone, and her synagogue was gone. So for her, there was no longer any there there. But just in case people want to check on that, now we have a statue at City Center called 'There.'"

Where the old pier once stood at the foot of Broadway, today you'll find Jack London Square. Famous for its shops and restaurants, Jack London Square is now a cultural mecca with concerts and many other events.

One of the biggest attractions of the square however, is decidedly basic and downright weathered: Jack London's cabin from the Klondike. "The cabin was situated in the Yukon Territory," says Barbara Moore, another volunteer walking tour guide. "Naturally, the Canadians wanted it, but the people in Oakland wanted it too. So a compromise was reached and

public life. Now, more than fifty years after his death, the spirit of FDR is still evident onboard.

Several days a month (March to November), the *Potomac* leaves its dock and cruises the bay on public tours. While at berth, the *Potomac* is open to the public twice a week (year-round). The yacht has been restored to look the way it did when Roosevelt was Commander-in-Chief, and yet the accommodations are relatively modest. FDR loved to entertain guests on the *Potomac*. "He was," says volunteer docent Dale Hansen, "by all reports, an extremely open and gregarious man who loved people."

Long before his presidential years, Roosevelt had been severely disabled by polio, so he adapted the ship to meet his physical needs. To carry him from deck to deck, an elevator was installed in one of the smokestacks. The President operated it using a rope and pulley. He could have put in an electric motor, but FDR also used the elevator as a form of exercise.

You can continue your walking tour of Oakland by swinging away from the waterfront toward downtown a few blocks. You'll discover that ambling through Oakland's earliest neighborhoods can be invigorating—and also delicious—if you stop at Ratto's on Washington Street between Eighth and Ninth Streets. Ratto's was founded as a basic grocery store by

Ratto & Co. International Grocers

Martin Durandi's grandfather back in 1897. His father added a European touch. When Martin took over in 1954, he added more international products—everything from Chilean mushrooms to Egyptian green wheat. One of the best things about Ratto's is the smell. The combination of spices, cheeses, and all the other food creates an unforgettable aroma.

Today the family tradition at Ratto's is continuing for a fourth generation. Martin has handed the reins to his daughter Elena. And though she'll undoubtedly put her own mark on the place, the spirit

of Ratto's won't change anytime soon.

Just beyond Ratto's front door is the diverse neighborhood of Ninth Street. If it's Friday between 8 A.M. and 2 P.M. you're in luck, because the Old Oakland Farmers Market closes Ninth Street to traffic, and opens it to edible exploration.

During the market hours, Ninth Street is transformed from the ordinary into the exotic. It becomes part circus, part supermarket, and part cultural classroom. It's a smorgasbord of sights, sounds, and smells that reminds cooking instructor Kasma Loha-Unchit of her native Thailand. "It's a lot like markets in Southeast Asia," says Kasma, "because it's open and very festive."

Kasma gives Thai cooking classes to the public and buys many of her ingredients at the farmers' market. "We have Filipino farmers here, we have Hmong farmers here, and we have Hispanic farmers," Kasma explains. "And then you have . . . other Northern California farmers also."

Staples and delicacies of many kinds give color to the market and pleasure to your palate. You're encouraged to nibble your way from one end of the market to the other, tasting the world along the way.

After you've stocked up on of international foodstuffs and made the rounds, your feet might tire. Why not consider doing something really different, like touring the Bay Area by air aboard a historic plane?

From the Kaiser Air Terminal near the Oakland International Airport, you can fly on a C-41—a military version of the famous DC-3s that have been workhorses of aviation since 1935. Today, the plane touring the Bay Area is owned by Otis Spunkmeyer Air—the cookie people. It's available for charters, or you can buy a ticket on a scheduled sky tour. But during World War II it was the flying command headquarters for the legendary General Hap Arnold. It's been restored to its original Army Air Corps glory, and in 1994 it even flew across the Atlantic for the fiftieth anniversary of D-Day.

Flying in this piece of history, you get high enough to see the whole Bay Area, but close enough to see the details. Jim Findlay pilots this classic aircraft, and he loves to watch the reactions of passengers. "I see them going back and forth from window to window," says Jim. "They can't get enough of it. They see a view they've never seen before and they just soak it in like a sponge."

Whether you take an organized walking tour of Oakland or just set out on your own; whether you linger at Ratto's, the saloon, Roosevelt's yacht, or the farmers' market; take to the air; or encounter some new discovery, it's all a part of the rich tapestry that makes Oakland the vibrant and diverse city it is.

Oakland Walking Tours 510-238-3234
USS *Potomac* 510-839-8256
Ratto & Co. International Grocers
510-832-6503
Old Oakland Farmers' Market
510-745-7100
Kasma Loha-Unchit 510-655-8900
http://users.lanminds.com/
~kasma-good
Otis Spunkmeyer Air 800-938-1900

Otis Spunkmeyer C-41

NILES CANYON:
Steaming
into the Past

There's a place in the Bay Area where the last spike may have been hammered into a rough-hewn redwood tie to complete the transcontinental railroad. It's a place where you can still hear the beautiful sound of steam locomotives. It's also a

City of Niles, "Hollywood" sign

place where California's most notorious bandit once roamed and where you can find a quiet little town that could have been Hollywood. The place is Niles Canyon, situated east of Fremont and west of Sunol, between Interstate 880 and 680 about an hour's drive from San Francisco.

A lovely creek runs through the canyon, and so do historic trains steaming back into the region's rich history. Niles Canyon is a picturesque place to visit and the old trains are fun to ride. The whole experience is pure time capsule, where the past is preserved.

The trains are lovingly restored and operated by volunteers like Alan Ramsey. Alan takes great pleasure in passing along the legends of the canyon. "This section of track through the canyon was the last of the original transcontinental railroad that was completed. They drove the last spike at Niles on September 6, 1869. They had no ceremony, and it was just a regular iron spike. In fact, we've got no proof of exactly where the last spike was driven."

Local history buff Phil Holmes adds, "For sure they drove the last spike some-place between here and San Leandro. But we don't know where for sure." Not surprisingly, people from Niles believe the last spike was pounded in or near their town; people from San Leandro claim it

> "All I need to make a comedy is a park, a policeman, and a pretty girl."
>
> CHARLIE CHAPLIN,
> My Autobiography, 1964

was closer to their town. Regardless of the exact location, the friendly rivalry is eclipsed by the collective pride in the region's railroading legacy.

Another local legacy tells of Joaquin Murieta, the notorious bandit who robbed and killed miners during California's Gold Rush period. Alan Ramsey will tell you that Murieta had his ranch in Los Molinos down at the mouth of Niles Canyon. But Ramsey says Murieta wasn't a bandit here in Niles. In fact, he was downright friendly. When Captain Harry Love claimed to have gunned down Murieta near Coalinga in 1853, authorities put his head in a jar—along with Three-Fingered Jack's right hand—as gruesome proof that the elusive Murieta and his compadre finally met their match. But local legends say it wasn't Murieta's head, and that the famed bandit lived peacefully in Niles Canyon for the rest of his life as a gentleman rancher.

Colorful characters have long moved through this equally colorful canyon. But some of Niles' early history is preserved in black and white. In fact, Niles was the original Hollywood. Charlie Chaplin filmed *The Tramp* here more than eighty years ago. And from 1912 through 1916, Bronco Billy Anderson created what were probably the first movie images of the Wild West in Niles.

According to Phil, Bronco Billy wasn't handsome and he didn't know how to ride, rope, fight, or shoot. He is credited instead with creating the "stunt double"—someone who took his place on the screen for all the cowboy tricks. "He was not the most talented actor," says Phil with a chuckle, "I'm sure of that." But, for a while, he was the most successful, and built the first studio on the West Coast, and signed on actors such as Charlie Chaplin.

But Billy and Charlie differed from one another and made strange bedfellows. Bronco Billy could wrap up one of his Westerns in two days, then disappear to San Francisco for fun and parties. Chaplin was an artist; he would take more than three weeks to create a film, keeping a keen eye on all aspects of production. Many believe that the time he spent in Niles actually made Chaplin. He was a famous comedian when he came here; when he left he was the world's most famous comedian.

And even though Niles lost its studio business to Hollywood, it wasn't without

Train bridge, Niles Canyon

its Hollywood-style scandals. Chaplin was the principal cause of the town's most lasting uproar. At one point during his Niles career he moved into a house in town with a woman without being married. "That was a problem in those days," smiles Phil Holmes, "a very serious problem. The neighborhood was all upset about that." But in Niles, scandals came and went pretty quickly, and so did Chaplin and the movies. All went south to Hollywood around 1916. Bronco Billy lost his financing and his studio; Niles lost its claim to future moviemaking fame.

The trains—the Niles time machines—know these secrets. And the people of all ages who ride have a ball. So do the volunteers who drive them, maintain them, and keep alive the romance of the rails.

Mac McAllister is another one of those volunteers. "As Johnny Cash said, 'I've got a thing about trains,'" says Mac.

Mac can't resist the sound of the rails. He even dreams about trains at night, and he remembers the stories his railroading father told him decades ago. "You know," continues Mac, "when you introduce a kid to a steam engine, maybe thirty years from now he'll remember fondly that, 'Oh gee, when I was a little kid, my folks took me out and I saw this steam locomotive.' It's what happened to me, and the rest is history."

Niles Canyon Railroad, Pacific Locomotion Association 510-862-9063

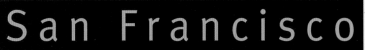

San Francisco

From left: The corner of Haight and Ashbury (Tour 37),
the Carême Room (Tour 36),
and the Cable Car Museum (Tour 35)

THE GOLDEN GATE NATIONAL RECREATION AREA:
An Unparalleled Bay Area Treasure

The Golden Gate National Recreation Area (GGNRA) is the country's most diverse urban national park. The Golden Gate Bridge itself is at the heart of this vast and complex park spanning three counties—from the edge of Tomales Bay in West Marin to the Phleger Estate just north of Woodside on the Peninsula.

In between these two sites, the park includes the open hillsides of the Marin Headlands, the raw cliffs of San Francisco's Lands End, a Civil War–era fortress, a historic military base, a notorious prison, and many miles of sparkling beaches.

"This park is so wonderful," says park Superintendent Brian O'Neill, "because

Golden Gate Bridge and the Marin Headlands from the Presidio

depending on how you feel, and what you need, and what's important at that point in your life, the park has just about everything to offer."

The lands of the GGNRA have everything, from some of the tallest and oldest trees on earth to delicate little plants on the verge of extinction; from wide-open vistas to the inner recesses of historic buildings. The park is perfect for kids; thousands of children who love to learn visit the Discovery Museum on the Bay every year.

"I think we're the envy of many cities in this country and around the world," says Brian, "because such an amazing resource exists among a population of six million people."

Close to twenty million people visit the park each year and contribute about $500 million to the region's economy. Ranger Brett Bankie believes they get their money's worth. "People from the interior of the country," says Brett, "come out here and see the ocean for the first time, they look out over the Pacific and the Golden Gate Bridge, and they just say 'Wow!'"

Best of all, the GGNRA is within a few minutes of most of our homes. The park is so accessible that it's easy to take it for granted, but we shouldn't. It is a gift to all of us from many dedicated people who

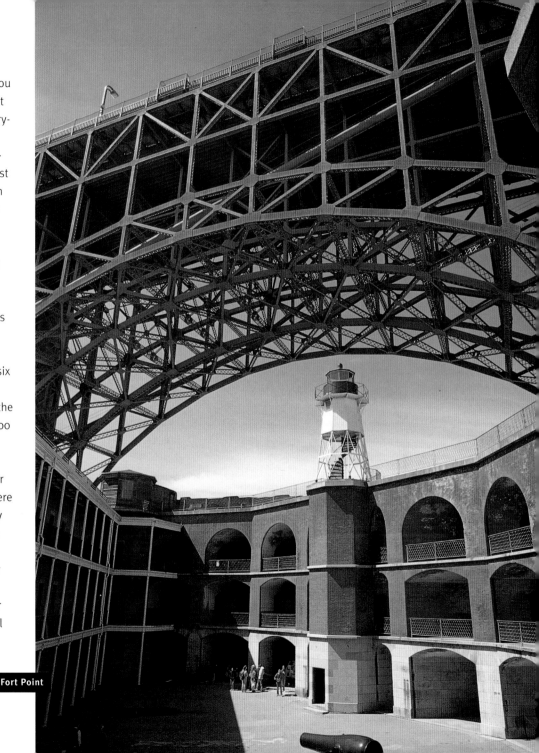

Fort Point

worked hard to assemble the system and save it from being overrun by development.

One of *Bay Area Backroads*' favorite historic sites within the GGNRA is the Civil War–era Fort Point, nestled underneath the Golden Gate Bridge's southern span. The fort was very nearly torn down when the bridge was built in 1937, but fortunately the bridge's main engineer fell in love with the old landmark and designed

The National Cemetery in the Presidio

a special archway to keep the fort intact. Today Fort Point is open Wednesday through Sunday for everyone to enjoy, and it's very popular with school groups.

Fort Point is the oldest brick fort west of the Mississippi. It was completed in 1861—when Lincoln was president—and stood in defense of San Francisco Bay in case of Confederate attack. San Francisco was the gateway to the gold country and its vast wealth was coveted by the Confederacy. But the fort's cannons never had to be fired, because the attacks never materialized.

Ranger William Johnson is grateful to be stationed at the fort. "It's a beautiful example of the mason's art," he explains. "More than eight million bricks were used in the construction of the fort. It's a symbol of a bygone era that we'll never see again."

Next door to Fort Point is another, yet older, military compound—the San Francisco Presidio. The Presidio was originally established in 1776 by the Spanish, taken over by Mexico in 1822, and finally claimed by the U.S. in 1846. Today it's managed by the National Park Service.

The Presidio is more than one and a half times as big as Golden Gate Park, covering almost 5 percent of San Francisco's land mass. Its grounds are connected by some seventy miles of paved roads, dozens of miles of trails, and eight hundred buildings representing eighteen

styles of architecture. There are ample open spaces and scenic views across the Presidio, and it is also home to ecological restoration programs and several rare and endangered plant species.

First-time visitors might be surprised, but one of the Presidio's most scenic spots is the National Cemetery, situated just off Lincoln Boulevard. It dates back to 1850, and is now the final resting place for about thirty thousand people including veterans of every American war from the Civil War on. Continuing on Lincoln Boulevard, you'll come across the Presidio's Museum (at Funston Avenue). At the museum, open Wednesday through Sunday, you can learn more about the history of the base by studying the exhibits and the artifacts on display.

Across Highway 101 from the museum is Crissy Field, presently the site of a habitat restoration project. Even though the field is undergoing a face lift, it is still open for running, biking, walking and windsurfing aficionados. More than seventy years ago Crissy Field—when it was a U.S. Army airfield—played a major role in the history of aviation. In 1924, the first dawn-to-dusk transcontinental flight ended here, and in the same year, the first round-the-world flight made one of its last stops at Crissy Field.

From the shoreline at Crissy Field, visitors to the GGNRA have an excellent view

Alcatraz

of America's most infamous prison—Alcatraz. But don't settle for just a view; hop on a ferry at Pier 41 and go on a tour of "the Rock." Today, Alcatraz is visited by one million people a year, but it has not always been such a desired destination. In 1852, the first lighthouse on the West Coast was built here, and a year later a

military fort was built on top of this barren island to guard the bay and California's gold. Soon, a citadel was constructed to house soldiers and their families, soil was carried over from the mainland, and Alcatraz was transformed into a lush, though somewhat lonely, fortress surrounded by gardens.

In 1934, Alcatraz began its most well-

known career as a high-security federal prison for some of the nation's most hardened criminals—Al "Scarface" Capone, George "Machine Gun" Kelly, Alvin "Creepy" Carpas, and the "Birdman" Robert Stroud. Wherever prisoners looked, they saw a guard with a gun looking down at them. But the ultimate punishment was the Hole—solitary confinement.

The prison was closed in 1963, and it soon began to fall into ruin. In 1972 the island became part of the GGNRA, and during those intervening years, Alcatraz grew wild. The island's imported vegetation has flourished and now Alcatraz is a critical nesting site for cormorants, gulls, black-crowned night herons, and other birds—an unlikely refuge in the heart of the Bay. Today you can be "locked" in the Hole as part of the daily guided tours, learn about other aspects of the island's history, or simply enjoy the views.

People of all ages and backgrounds show their appreciation for the GGNRA in many ways. Some people do so by volunteering; they study the annual migration of hawks, build access trails so people who use wheelchairs can share in the park's treasures, or remove non-native plants so native species can flourish. But whether you feel the need to volunteer, get away, exercise, or learn some history, the Golden Gate National Recreation Area offers many rewards to those who visit.

Fort Point 415-556-1693
Presidio Visitor Center (for Museum)
   415-561-4323
Alcatraz (tour and ferry information)
   415-705-5555

Holy Trinity Orthodox Cathedral

SAN FRANCISCO'S
SACRED PLACES

34

If the truth be told, San Francisco was essentially founded on greed—people flocked here looking to get rich quick during the Gold Rush. But despite its raucous beginnings, the city has developed into quite a spiritual place. In many ways, our lives are still driven by the hectic quest for material wealth, but if we slow down and take the time to look, it's easy to find many sacred treasures hidden away on the backroads of San Francisco.

The sacred places of San Francisco are as diverse as the people who live here. There's Mission Dolores; the Tien Hau Temple in the heart of Chinatown—the oldest Chinese temple in the U.S.; and the venerable Vedanta Hindu Temple near the Marina District. There's also the Soto Zen Buddhist Mission in Japantown and St. John's African Orthodox Church in the Haight-Ashbury, where the music of John Coltrane is revered. These sites of worship have not only spiritual but also aesthetic and historic significance.

John Gaul is a local historian who spends much of his time leading tours at the Palace of Fine Arts. "There are a number of sacred places in San Francisco that I absolutely adore," admits John. "They express religion to me in an awe-inspiring way, but they're also extremely beautiful. And one of my favorite churches is the Holy Trinity Orthodox Cathedral."

The cathedral, on the corner of Van Ness and Green, was built in 1909. The parish was established back in 1857, and it's rich with history. The cathedral's chandelier was a gift of Nicholas the Second, the last Russian Czar. The church's magnificent bells were cast in 1888 at the behest of Nicholas's father, Alexander the Third. The largest of the bells weighs nearly three tons.

"People simply stop by and say how much they love our bells because it's a very joyful sound," says Father Victor Sokolov, Holy Trinity's priest. "In Russia we have a very good expression, that the temple is saturated with prayers, saturated with spirit. You can really feel it. And when you look at the artifacts, when you look at the icons, when you look at all those little precious objects around the temple, every one of them has gained history, and you know, every nail in the temple has its own history."

Another one of John's favorites is Congregation Sherith Israel. Martin Feldman has been cantor of Sherith Israel since 1960. "The structure is extraordinary," says Cantor Feldman. "Every time I open up my mouth—which is often—either in the singing or in talking or chanting or whatever I'm doing, I'm just in awe," he says. "I'm filled with great inspiration. I just close my eyes and I feel that I'm relating somehow to the metaphysical, whether it's to God or the history of the Jewish people or a combination."

The history of Sherith Israel closely parallels that of San Francisco. The congregation was formed during the Gold Rush and the first temple was built in 1854. The present building, constructed in 1904, was used by San Francisco's

John Gaul at Swedenborgian Church

Superior Courts for two years after the 1906 earthquake. Today the congregation is raising money to complete a costly earthquake retrofit.

Another interesting place of worship is tucked away behind walls at the corner of Lyon and Washington. It's the charming and rustic Swedenborgian Church, built in 1895. "The Swedenborgian Church has always been called the poetry of architecture," John notes.

Not only is the Swedenborgian Church poetic, it was the place for the baptism in the 1870s of one of the greatest poets—Robert Frost. And naturalist John Muir worshipped here, comfortable in a church designed in harmony with nature.

All of these places and many more around the city are open for visitors to experience—to gain an understanding of others' beliefs, to glimpse slices of the city's history, or simply to take in the sites' beauty. These buildings also serve as a reminder for us to take the time to find our own sacred places, whether they're inside houses of worship, along garden walkways, or out in nature.

Holy Trinity Orthodox Cathedral
    415-673-8565
Congregation Sherith Israel
    415-346-1720
Swedenborgian Church 415-346-6466

CABLE CARS:
The Original San Francisco Treat

Residents of the Bay Area are familiar with San Francisco's most famous symbol—the cable car. In fact, many of us hardly even notice them anymore. Cable cars are too often dismissed as tourist attractions, something locals just don't do. But the rest of the world finds cable cars fascinating and knows what we may have forgotten: these little cars lead to surprising urban backroads, to the very roots of San Francisco. Spending an afternoon with the cable cars can transport you to a world filled with the authentic sights, sounds, and smells of the city. In a place that celebrates the unique and unusual, these one-of-a-kind cars are a perfect fit.

Louis Montanyo is a cable car brake man and he typifies the lucky few who work on the cars. He's convinced he has the best job in the city. Louis always has fun on his shift, and makes sure everyone else on his car does, too. On a typical day you can find him joking with passengers, yelling at pedestrians, and giving the cabs a good ribbing.

While most people "riding the ropes" are tourists doing it just for fun, a few San Franciscans commute to work via cable cars. Even the commuters get into the swing of things once aboard. "You have to show your Fast Pass," jokes downtown worker Doug Linden, "so people don't confuse you with the tourists."

One hundred and twenty years ago, this was San Francisco's mass transit system. The first cable car rode through San Francisco in 1873. Twenty-two cable lines were built around the city and replaced the messy, cruel, and often dangerous horsecars that dominated city streets at that time. The system's history is now preserved at the Cable Car Museum at 1201 Mason Street.

Merrill Cohn, a former city engineer and a serious cable car buff, volunteers at the museum. "When the big earthquake and fire happened in 1906," says Merrill, "one of the principal victims was the cable car system. It was almost lost forever, but it survived." After the earthquake the cable car system was partially rebuilt, but restrictive costs and the invention of electric trolleys meant the heyday of the cable car was over.

Earthquakes weren't the only threat to the cable cars, however. In 1946, city officials wanted to replace them with more modern buses. Enraged residents worked to put the issue on the ballot in 1947. "The citizens of San Francisco voted to keep the cable cars," says Merrill, "and that's why we have these lines today."

Cable cars at Hyde Street turnaround

Some of the heroes of that battle are honored at the museum, beside dozens of other exhibits. The facility is not only a museum, but also the nerve center and powerhouse of the cable car system. "We have four cables," explains Merrill, "one for each street that the cable cars travel: Powell, Mason, Hyde, and California."

Nearly twenty-five miles of churning metal cables are spun out into tunnels under the streets, pulling the cars along their routes. Today, only three of the original twenty-two lines remain, taking riders through distinct neighborhoods steeped in personality, color, and history—much like the cars themselves. "You go through

the Financial District, Chinatown, and you can ride a car down to the front of the Fairmont Hotel," Merrill boasts. "You can see a lot of the city just touring on the cable car."

Each of the cars is a rolling masterpiece; no two are exactly alike. Today cable cars are carefully crafted in a workshop on Potrero Hill, the only one of its kind. "It takes about eighteen months to build a cable car from start to finish," says John Stenson, the superintendent. "And that's basically one carpenter working on it full time. These are the Rolls Royces of the city's Muni Railway. Everything is hand-built. We're participating in San Francisco history," continues John. "These cable cars will be around for the next one hundred years. Your children and

Glen Hunsicker (left) and Dave Valstad at the cable car workshop

great-grandchildren will be able to ride on these. That's the nice part about actually working on cable cars."

And the nice part about driving them is the camaraderie. Conductor Duane Allen and brake man Arthur Stone have been rolling around San Francisco together for several years. Duane collects the fares and controls the rear brake. Arthur operates the cable grip and main brakes. "It takes years of experience," says Arthur, "and the guy I'm working with is one of the best, but I'm not going to tell him that!"

They work together on opposite ends of the car, keeping in contact the way brake men and conductors have for more than one hundred years: by using bells. "For instance," says Duane, "if we were going down a hill and Art needed more brakes, he would give me two rings with the bell."

The cable cars rumble along their tracks, leading to renowned landmarks and little-known corners of the city. They pull passengers back and forth along backroads that exist nowhere else on earth.

San Francisco Cable Car Museum

415-474-1887
http://www.artcom.com/museums/vs/sz/94108-10.htm

CALIFORNIA CULINARY ACADEMY: A Tasty Tour

Everyone knows that San Francisco is a great place for fine dining. The city draws on Northern California's agricultural riches and excellent wines and the spirit of a people always willing to try something new. The result is that eating here has become as much of a tourist attraction as cable cars. So, it should come as no surprise that San Francisco is also the home of a highly respected institution that teaches the culinary arts.

The California Culinary Academy, located at the corner of Polk and Turk Streets, was originally the German Cultural Arts Center. Now it's the home of two restaurants, twelve kitchens, and more than seven hundred aspiring chefs. The focus of the Academy is an eighteen-month culinary arts degree program.

The two restaurants are open to the public for lunch and dinner. The majestic Carême Room features a constantly evolving menu, where lunch entrées are reasonably priced. The more informal Tavern on the Tenderloin offers American specialties.

The food is prepared and served by students, but the Academy's Dan Homsey

Carême Room

says the food here is better than at most restaurants. "A lot of people think, 'Oh, we're eating their homework,' but you have to understand that when students are in the Academy's production courses they already have had months of training. They are each individually supervised by the chef instructor. All the product is tested and tasted before it comes out."

Pastry chef instructor Reg Elgin has a lot of fun with his job, but he takes it very seriously as well. "If I can put love and respect into every one of my recipes," Reg

Kitchen classroom at the California Culinary Academy

explains, "if I can put humor and a good time into each recipe, then I'm not going to produce anything less than perfect."

The eighteen-month Culinary Arts program may be financially exhausting—it costs about $25,000—but it's physically exhausting, too. Students attend classes seven hours a day, five days a week. If you do come to study here, Dan Homsey has some advice. "Take your brain out of your head, squeeze it like a sponge so it's completely dry, and then for the next eighteen months, absorb as much as possible. Because there is no way that you can possibly know as much as the chefs in these classrooms do in your lifetime."

You don't need to have a culinary career in mind to appreciate the Academy. Individual hands-on classes are offered to the public on Saturdays. You can also arrange to take a free tour of the facility. And if you eat in the Carême Room you can see right into the kitchen where your food is being prepared.

Whether you come to the Academy as a student or a day visitor, be sure to grab a bite to eat—a great deal no matter how you slice it.

The California Culinary Academy
415-771-3536
The Carême Room and the Tavern on the Tenderloin 415-292-8229

THE MANY FACES OF HAIGHT-ASHBURY

Back in the mid-1960s, San Francisco's Haight-Ashbury was perhaps the most famous intersection in the country. Back then, young people came from all over the world in search of love and peace. Some found it and some didn't, but that was only one chapter in this neighborhood's long and colorful history.

The *Backroads* crew caught up with Rachel Heller, who gives walking tours of the Haight. The Haight-Ashbury Walking Tours begin at the Stanyan Park Hotel at the corner of Stanyan and Waller, where a stadium once stood. In 1892, it was the site of the very first Cal-Stanford Big Game. "The people filled up the stands and the teams went out on the field to start the game," says Rachel, "and then they realized that neither team had remembered to bring a football!" At that time, the Haight was the far western edge of the city, and somebody had to go all the way back into town to get a ball.

Some residential streets in the Haight are lined with homes steeped in local lore. Rachel points to some well-maintained Victorians on Belvedere Street. "This whole row of houses are 1890 Cranston and Keenans. Cranston, as in

Cranston and Keenan Victorians

The corner of Haight and Ashbury

former Senator Alan Cranston. It was his grandfather who built some of the nicest Victorians in the city."

Some of the classic homes in the Haight have gained notoriety in more recent times. "This is the Grateful Dead House beside this 1890 Cranston-Keenan Victorian," Rachel points out, on Ashbury Street. "They lived here in the mid-sixties, all together. It's actually on the cover of one of their albums with them posing on the steps."

Sometimes when you walk around this neighborhood, it's as if time has stood still since the sixties. The cars, the shops, and even some of the tie-dye-clad people, seem as if they're only visiting the present day as tourists. Psychedelic oil lamps bubble slowly in store windows, and incense is in the air.

Stannous Flouride is a self-described writer, illustrator, designer, and trouble-maker. He created his own "star" map of the Haight, and he helps out with the walking tours. When asked if his name is really Stannous Flouride, he replies, "Well, reality is such a confining concept, don't you think?"

One of Stannous's favorite spots to show off is the corner of Waller and Cole. "I call this the macabre corner," he says with a wry smile. "A guy by the name of Charlie Manson lived in a garage here in a broken-down van. It was about 1967. Ol' X forehead himself."

Not all of Stan's surprises are unpleasant ones. "I'm going to show you something that's a family secret in the Haight-Ashbury." Stan leans over a nondescript sidewalk and points to the signature of John Lennon preserved in concrete—"John Lennon 12/5/69."

"At that time, he was here," states Stan. "He was staying with the Jefferson Airplane in their house a few blocks from here. Think about it. I mean, John Lennon was the kind of guy who would stop and write his name in wet cement."

The Haight is also the neighborhood where the Red Victorian flourishes. It's not just a bed-and-breakfast inn, it's also a peace center where people come to meditate and explore their potential. Cheryl Canfield is the Peace Center's Director. "That's part of our idealism here at the center," says Cheryl, "to create that kind of place where we can inspire people to get in touch with what they can do in the world."

If you simply want a quiet night's sleep, you can find that at the Red Vic, too. "Our rooms are done in themes of the Summer of Love, and we like to hold on to the idealism that came out of that time," explains Cheryl. All eighteen rooms are different. You'll find everything from the Flower Child Room to the Redwood Forest Room to the Japanese Tea Garden Room. Even the bathrooms are unique; one is called The Aquarium.

For Cheryl, this neighborhood is the perfect setting to motivate people to have a positive impact on society. For Stannous Flouride, it's where he's been experimenting with being who he is for decades. "I'm the only member of my family who moved out of Massachusetts in the last 270 years. I could never live there again. I mean, I've discovered paradise." For Rachel, it's a good community in which to raise her family and to dispel myths. "I'm not a hippie," she says with a smile, "and I live in this neighborhood!"

There's no doubt that fascination with the hippie era is the major draw for visitors to the Haight-Ashbury. But if you scratch beneath the surface, there's a broader picture to uncover. The Summer of Love was only one of more than a hundred summers that have given the Haight its color.

Haight-Ashbury Walking Tours
  415-863-1621
Stannous Flouride, Occasional Tours and Maps 415-552-8269
The Red Victorian Bed and Breakfast and Peace Center 415-864-1978

CALIFORNIA ACADEMY OF SCIENCES:
San Francisco's Institution of Science and Discovery

38

Many generations of Bay Area schoolchildren have first discovered the wonders of science at a very special place—the California Academy of Sciences. In Golden Gate Park, the imposing edifice is three museums in one—the Steinhart Aquarium, the Morrison Planetarium, and the Natural History Museum—explaining and celebrating the diversity of the ocean, space, and earth. The staff has worked hard to make the experience as interactive as possible by minimizing glass enclosures and simple pictures on the walls.

Steinhart Aquarium is home to more than 1,400 species of fresh and saltwater fish, who share the premises with their amphibian friends. Visitors come face-to-face with exotic moray eels, local leopard sharks, and other aquatic animals.

The Planetarium houses Northern California's largest indoor universe, where you can stargaze with an expert in the middle of the day and you never have to worry about the fog.

In the Natural History Museum, you'll see the earth's amazing creatures—from

Alligators at the Steinhart Aquarium

intimidating sea monsters that live in a tiny drop of sea water to the largest beasts that inhabited the planet.

The Academy of Sciences is more than just a local museum; it's the oldest scientific institution west of the Mississippi. The museum was founded in 1853 as a "Smithsonian of the West." It's been conducting scientific research ever since.

Dr. Bob Drewes is the chairman and curator of the Academy's Herpetology Department, which studies reptiles and amphibians. "I do for a living what I've wanted to do since I was four years old," he says. "I run around in swamps and catch things. And I also get to try and figure them out. That's the science part."

Bob has been studying reptiles and amphibians around the globe for twenty-seven years. "Most of the dioramas, the big ones in African Hall, are real places. I can point to mountains in some of these exhibits and tell you their names." As a child Bob remembers walking into the African Hall and saying "Wow! I've got to be here." The enthusiasm first sparked here hasn't diminished one bit. "Finding something new," says Bob, "be it a new species or a new way of looking at something or a new concept—literally transcends all other joys I can think of."

The Academy's first home was on

Pendulum clock in the Natural History Museum

Market Street in downtown San Francisco, in a building bequeathed by local millionaire James Lick. In 1906, the earthquake and fire destroyed the building, along with most of the collections and exhibits. The Academy relocated to Golden Gate Park in 1916, where it remains today.

In closed chambers throughout the Academy more than fourteen million individual animal and plant specimens of all kinds are cataloged and stored for scientists to study. Some of the species represented no longer exist, and their stored DNA information might prove valuable to future research. Just on the other side of the wall the "front room" of the Academy is where the public sees the work of scientists such as Bob.

If the scientists like Bob are the producers and directors of the show, then clearly the animals are the stars—from the cute and cuddly to some of the most feared predators on the planet. Senior Aquatic Biologist Ken Howell oversees many of the Academy's animals, including the alligator pond near the front of the Steinhart Aquarium. "These animals have all lived here together for many years. It's one happy family," says Ken. This "happy family" includes a pair of American alligators and nine alligator snapping turtles.

Nearby, you can find some of the deadliest snakes in the world—pythons, cobras, vipers, and Eastern Diamondback rattlers. These reptilian cousins require our respect and a little caution. Jim O'Brien is an aquatic biologist who cares for the snakes. "It's no different than working with power tools or with live electricity," says Jim nonchalantly. "We use hooks and tongs, and treat them much as you would a live piece of spaghetti."

Carey Linder is an aquatic biologist who has come to know some African black-footed penguins pretty well over the years. "I think they're a lot like people," says Carey, "because they have very individual personalities." Pierre the penguin, for example, is an eating machine. Grendal is picky; he only eats herring.

The trust that has developed between Carey and these penguins is crucial for the health of both creature and caretaker. But in some relationships, trust is overrated. Just ask aquatic biologist Lloyd Gomez—part of Lloyd's duties include caring for the resident reef sharks. "Trust is something humans like to do," Lloyd says with a smile, "but I wouldn't trust these guys."

Although Lloyd is wary of the sharks, he gets closer to them than most of us would ever dare. He keeps the sharks fat, happy, and healthy with the help of a pole and plenty of fish. These prehistoric creatures—widely viewed as mean or evil— are misunderstood. "They aren't mean at all," explains Lloyd, "they're a perfect eating machine. They were designed

Dr. Luis Baptista

to eat and that's what they do best."

Dr. Luis Baptista, chairman and curator of the Academy's Ornithology and Mammology Departments, has spent much of his life studying birds. Although he has traveled around the world to do so, some of his most important discoveries have resulted from information gathered just outside the Academy's doors.

Luis has learned that birds of the same species speak different languages, or dialects. "Like a Cockney English," says Luis, "or a New York person, or somebody from Brooklyn." For example, a white-crowned sparrow right outside of the Academy makes a slightly different call than a white-crowned sparrow near Elk Glen Lake, just a mile away.

Luis's knowledge of birds is staggering. "I could go to different parts of San Francisco," says Luis, "and if you blindfold me, I could probably tell you what part of San Francisco I'm in, just by the accent of the birds."

The work that goes on at the Academy of Sciences can help us see and hear the world in new ways. The Academy is a place where curiosity is encouraged, passions are born, and new discoveries are still being made every day.

California Academy of Sciences
   415-750-7145
Behind-the-Scenes Tours 415-750-7247

Mural restoration at Flynn Elementary School

MURALS IN THE MISSION:
Artwork for and by the People

San Francisco has long attracted talented artists of all kinds. It's home to many wonderful art museums and galleries. But the Mission District also nurtures its artists. In fact, the entire neighborhood is like one big outdoor museum, and it's always open.

There are more than a hundred murals in the Mission District. Many are the work of the Precita Eyes Mural Arts Center. The Precita Eyes Center encourages artists of all ages with a wide range of classes and programs. The center also puts together weekly mural walks.

"My feeling is that the murals themselves are so eloquent that what I say is almost irrelevant," says tour leader Patricia Rose, a muralist herself. The murals are eloquent and incredibly diverse—in both style and subject matter. Some murals have overtly political messages; others express themes of family and community.

The mural locations are also varied; a laundromat, the entrance to a swimming pool, a bank lobby, even the exterior of a PG&E plant. "It's something this

Susan Cervantes restoring a mural at Flynn Elementary School

121

community really responds to," says Patricia. "People appreciate them and are very proud of them, too."

Murals seem to draw out even the most reticent observers. Once Patricia was painting Chinese zodiac symbols in a mural outside a Chinese restaurant when one of the restaurant's employees noticed something missing from her snake. "He was watching really intently and finally he said, 'Ah,' and stuck out his tongue, you know, as if to say 'This is what you need,'" recalls Patricia. "And when I put in a tiny little line for the tongue, he was so happy! This man had never spoken a word of English to us, but then started nodding his head saying, 'Yes, yes, yes.'"

Nowhere are murals more integrated into the neighborhood than in tiny, one-block-long Balmy Alley. Nancy Ippolito lives on Balmy Alley. Her garage is adorned with a striking mural painted by children who have been affected by AIDS. "It's exciting, partly because you get to see the artwork everyday, and it's also exciting to see the kind of attention it gets," says Nancy. "People will be standing here, talking about what a thrill it is to come here and look at this."

Elba Rivera found her home on Balmy Alley when she was helping paint a mural across the street. "I was enjoying this

alley," says Elba, "because people would come by here and make suggestions about the mural like 'Oh, ah, you don't have Cuba quite right; I'll bring you a map.' People were just wonderfully warm."

One of the community's most beautiful murals stretches out on the walls of Cesar Chavez Elementary on Shotwell Street. Not only does Nancy's daughter attend the school, but Elba worked on the mural. "That was neat," says Elba, "because that's where I went to school as a kid!"

The Precita Eyes Mural Arts Center has influence beyond the Mission District. Susan Cervantes works at the Center, and you can often find her supervising groups of budding artists, like an enthusiastic group of third graders from Chinatown's Commodore-Stockton School. They painted a mural in their playground. "Every single kid has a design in this mural," says Susan. "So they all feel that they're a part of it, and not separate from it. So it's really truly their mural."

Susan founded Precita Eyes in 1977. A lot of murals in the Mission District bear her signature, including the awe-inspiring mural that covers the Women's Building on Eighteenth Street. "They wanted us to do a little tiny mural on the side of the

building," remembers Susan, "because that's all they had funding for. But when you get together a bunch of painters, that won't do. So the first meeting we had, we decided we were going to go for the whole thing."

The art of the Mission extends to places like the Mission Cultural Center on Mission Street between Twenty-fourth and Twenty-fifth. It has its own art classes and exhibits. At Galeria de la Raza on Twenty-fourth Street, and its folk art store Studio 24, the artwork of the Mission District is on display and for sale. "Maybe you'll learn about something you never saw before," says archivist Olivia Armas, "and you'll learn to appreciate differences. Or maybe you're a Latino or Chicano and you'll walk in here and say, 'Casa, casa, esto es mi casa!'"

That's also the hope of the folks at Precita Eyes, to maintain a supportive environment for local artists—young and old—and to expose the rest of us to a neighborhood that is essentially a living art gallery.

Precita Eyes Walking Tour 415-285-2287
The Mission Cultural Center 415-821-1155
Galeria de la Raza/Studio 24
415-826-8009

Peninsula and South Bay

From left: View of Santa Clara Valley from Mount Hamilton (Tour 42) and Loma Mar Post Office (Tour 43)

PACIFICA:
The Bay Area's Little-Known Coastal Town

When people from the Bay Area want to go to the coast, they usually think of Marin, Point Reyes, Mendocino, Santa Cruz, Monterey, or even Big Sur. But there's another terrific coastal area that usually gets overlooked. It's just south of San Francisco, in the little town of Pacifica.

Highway One cuts right through the middle of Pacifica, some fifteen miles south of the Golden Gate Bridge. Instead of just driving through, it's worth stopping for a closer look. You'll find some surprises, and some very interesting people. Pacifica has a reputation for raucous politics—and heavy fog. Some people think Pacifica could be called the Fog Capital of the Pacific Coast. If you ask most locals, though, they'll tell you it's a myth. Whether you reach Pacifica on a day obscured by fog or lit up with sun, you're bound to find a wealth of things to see and do. Pacifica is home to beautiful beaches, numerous parks, and a very popular fishing pier.

It must have been a clear day in 1769 when Don Gaspar de Portolá made the first recorded discovery of San Francisco Bay. He passed through what is now Pacifica and first saw the bay from nearby Sweeny Ridge. One hundred and eighty-eight years later, in 1957, Pacifica became a city when nine communities banded together. Some are right on the coast, while others are in narrow valleys surrounded by steep mountains.

Nick Gust is a former mayor of Pacifica and owner of Nick's Restaurant. He loves to show off his town, especially the little isolated neighborhood called Shelter Cove off San Pedro Avenue. "The people that live here have to carry everything in," explains Nick. "They can't drive in at all; there's no access. It's about a half a mile from where they park their cars."

Another hidden treasure lies at the end of a typical suburban street. Bud Butler's Park Pacifica Stables are a little slice of the Wild West, and Bud welcomes visitors. "Come by and take a look at my horses," says Bud. "Most days when there's fog on the coast, we have sunshine back here."

Nearly half of the land in Pacifica is open space, including the Golden Gate National Recreation Area, the San Pedro Valley County Park, and Pacifica State Beach. At Rockaway Beach, famous for surfing and for restaurants like Nick's and the Moonraker, the sunsets are unparalleled—when the fog has fled the coast. There are also golf courses, shops, and the Sanchez Adobe, built more than

Sam's Castle

one hundred and fifty years ago. There's even the Shelldance Nursery with orchids and the largest collection of bromeliads in the West.

Pacificans have stories to tell about the town's colorful past, especially when it was a haven for bootleggers and when the Sanchez Adobe was a speakeasy. But there's also a good story about Christmas,

1963. "What happened was all the kids were lined up in the shopping center parking lot and Santa Claus parachuted in," remembers one resident, "and all of a sudden the wind caught him and he just drifted into the ocean. The kids all ran across the road toward the beach. Luckily a surfer brought Santa in, and he was still able to give away candies!"

Perhaps one of Pacifica's most famous landmarks is Sam's Castle. It was built back in 1908 as a family home by the grandfather of the former congressman Pete McCloskey. San Simeon might have the Hearst Castle, but Pacifica is proud of its equivalent.

Sam Mazza is the king of this castle.

Pacifica coastline

He has crammed ornate furniture, religious artifacts, suits of armor, chandeliers, porcelain statues, decorative screens, and who knows what else, into twenty rooms on four floors of this brick castle with a terrific view of the Pacifica coast.

Sam says he came to own the place on a lark. "I took my girlfriend out to breakfast and we had some gin fizzes. And I felt no pain so we took a drive down the highway to Pacifica. And I saw this pile of bricks and stones and it looked interesting so I just thought I'd buy it."

Sam bought the castle in 1958 for $29,000. He doesn't live in it, but he visits on the weekends from his home in San Francisco. Sam worked as a theater decorator for 20th Century Fox most of his life and over the years he acquired treasures that were being thrown out of some of the finest movie houses in California.

"So," remarks Sam with a smile, "it's just a kind of fun house." Sam's Castle is a private residence and not open to the public, but you can see the castle from the Sharp Park State Beach area. The castle is located in the hills above Pacifica, where the fog is either a frequent visitor or a piece of mythology, depending on how you see things.

Pacifica Chamber of Commerce
650-355-4122

DRAWBRIDGE:
Lessons Learned from a Once-Thriving Town

Both for longtime residents of the Bay Area and for newcomers, the idea of a ghost town in our midst comes as a real surprise. But if you venture down to the southern portion of the Bay and the magnificent nineteen thousand-acre San Francisco Bay National Wildlife Refuge, you'll find such a place. It is called Drawbridge.

Today Drawbridge—a gathering of gray weathered buildings being reclaimed by nature—is a small marshy island north of San Jose and Santa Clara, about three miles from the town of Alviso, by Coyote Creek. But back in approximately 1876, people started venturing out here for the excellent hunting and fishing. The South Pacific Coast Railroad had just completed a rail line through the south bay's marshes and people could ride the rails to Drawbridge.

By the early twentieth century, Drawbridge had become a full-time community. On weekends, the population swelled with hunters and vacationers from surrounding cities. Because of its remote

Drawbridge

Docent Susan TenEyck at Drawbridge

location, and no local government or law enforcement, Drawbridge also attracted gambling, bootlegging, and brothels.

Barry Nelson, former Executive Director of the Save San Francisco Bay Association, knows this region well. He explains that before Drawbridge and the arrival of Europeans to the Bay, the area's native people flourished here. "One of the reasons there were more Native Americans around here than just about anyplace else in the Bay Area," says Barry, "was that life was pretty good. In the wintertime there were geese, in the fall the salmon were running, in the spring there were shorebirds, and year-round there were shellfish. Also, the weather was just as good for them as it is for us today."

Out on the Bay, or walking its shoreline on one of the refuge's many trails, it's

Drawbridge

easy to imagine yourself several hundred years ago in a tule raft like the Ohlone people once used. During migrations the sky would be filled with birds; early accounts tell of the Bay's sky darkened with flocks of migrating geese and waterfowl. Today's shorebird populations aren't as large, but even still, up to one million shorebirds pass through the Bay every year on their migratory travels up and down the Pacific flyway. Visitors to Drawbridge and the Wildlife Refuge can view everything from lumbering white pelicans to diminutive sanderlings.

Barry enjoys paddling out to Drawbridge from Fremont in a modern canoe (not a tule raft) through a maze of creeks and sloughs. You can do the same, or sign up for a guided tour of the island conducted by Wildlife Refuge volunteers.

John Steiner, former chief of education and interpretation for the San Francisco Bay National Wildlife Refuge, has led many tours of Drawbridge. John explains how families set up house on the north side of town, but the south side of town was a different story. "Legend has it that there was some wicked nightlife down at that end of town," says John with a wry smile. When conditions permitted residents had what they called "high-tide parties" when the water level allowed neighbors to tie up to each other's porches and partake in a kind of progres-

sive water-borne party. Because of the marshy ground and the high tides, all the houses were built on stilts and were connected to the railroad tracks by walkways. In the 1920s during its heyday Drawbridge had four hundred residents living in about ninety houses.

John has met some of the people who made this island their home. "They say it was difficult to live here because it was so remote. There were no services. There was no plumbing, there was no electricity. You pretty much had to fend for yourself." But, John says, they stayed because it was so beautiful: clean air, knock-your-socks-off vistas, a swimmable slough, and ducks everywhere.

Drawbridge became a ghost town when the habitat was ravaged. "It was destroyed very slowly," explains John. "By the 1940s there was raw sewage floating in the sloughs. No more swimming in the sloughs then. In fact, you could smell the sewage. That kept a lot of people away." Eventually, the fishing and shrimping industry vanished and the marshes were turned into landfills, airports, freeways, subdivisions, and shopping malls. By the 1950s, few residents remained. Wells ran dry and the island began to sink into the marsh. Many of the abandoned homes were vandalized, looted, and burned. The last resident left Drawbridge in 1979.

Barry believes that Drawbridge stands

as a testament to human folly and a warning about the perils of habitat loss. If we lost all the wetlands in San Francisco Bay it would mean certain death for tens of thousands of birds. It would be like a person trying to drive across the United States but discovering there weren't any gas stations in Utah or Colorado. Explaining the analogy, Barry claims, "the whole system would fall apart. You wouldn't be able to complete your trip, just like there would be no fuel for the birds to complete their amazing journeys." John agrees with Barry. "The lesson here is that the beautiful and productive environment attracted people, but then the people spoiled the local environment, the people left, and Drawbridge didn't survive."

Drawbridge is closed to the public because of the many hazards around the old structures (even canoe enthusiasts should contact the refuge for permission). However, you can see it on a tour every Saturday morning from May through October. You won't need to paddle a canoe, either; these tours get you close to the island by van, and then it's a short walk. Tours of Drawbridge are limited to thirteen people per week.

Drawbridge 510-792-0222
Save San Francisco Bay Association
510-452-9261

MOUNT HAMILTON AND THE JUNCTION: The Bay Area's Empty Quarter

Mount Hamilton is the towering gateway to one of the Bay Area's least populated regions. Strike out along Highway 130 in the Santa Clara Valley, just off Highway 101, and wind your way up to the mountain's 4,372-foot summit. The road meanders and corkscrews into a wonderful confusion of switchbacks and hairpin turns as you climb through a succession of inviting California landscapes: grassland, oak woodland, and mixed forest.

From the valley floor the mountain is very deceiving. It looms before you, seemingly just a stone's throw away, and yet the trip to the top takes about an hour from downtown San Jose. As you near the summit you'll see a startling sight: The fantastic spheres of the University of California's James Lick Observatory—the world's first permanently staffed modern observatory.

The Lick Observatory is actually a cluster of buildings housing some of the oldest—and some of the most modern—astronomical equipment watching over the cosmos today. Specialists from around the world come here to uncover the mysteries of the universe. But the observatory is more than a research facility; it's also one of the most unique villages in Northern California. In fact, it's a full-blown town with a fire station, a one-room schoolhouse, and a population of some fifty-five people. And, as in many small towns, the residents here play many roles.

Jack Schultz, the former superintendent of the Lick Observatory, explains that this scientific installation is more than machines and Ph.D.s. "It's like any small town community," says Jack. "We all know what's going on with each other almost immediately before it happens."

All this mountaintop life began with the construction of the first observatory in 1875. Its benefactor was San Franciscan James Lick. In the mid-1800s he gave money to what was going to be the University of California to "build the largest and finest telescope in the world."

Visitors to the observatory can see the mountain's original telescope and learn how astronomy was practiced in the old days, when water power lifted up the wooden floor fourteen feet to boost astronomers up to the telescope. The beautifully crafted dome and classic refracting telescope evoke images of astronomers shivering through long, cold

Lick Observatory on Mount Hamilton

A telescope at Lick Observatory

nights while peering into the heavens. Back then, before photography and computers, scientists had to write down what they observed. And yet much of our modern understanding of the universe was accomplished on the top of Mount Hamilton using these basic techniques.

These days astronomy is quite different. You can see this yourself on one of the daytime tours of the modern telescopes. When night falls astronomers emerge, like determined nocturnal creatures, to study the heavens from the comfort of their control rooms. Alex Filippenko, an astronomy professor at U.C. Berkeley, has spent many hours at the Lick Observatory. "Today," explains the star-gazing veteran, "it's all done digitally with computers, and in a warmer room. It's a lot more pleasant. Basically, we want to understand the process by which we came to be. We are, as Carl Sagan said, made of star stuff. Every atom in your body, aside from hydrogen and trace quantities of helium, came from exploding stars."

It is hard to part with the joys of Mount Hamilton, but as Highway 130 slithers like an asphalt sidewinder down toward Livermore and the Bay Area's empty quarter, you'll soon realize you're leaving one adventure and starting a new one. Just like the west side of the mountain,

The Junction

she never makes a sale. "If I sell it, I sell it. If I don't, I don't," says Ruthie with a throaty laugh. "I even tried to sell my husband once, and it almost worked!" The real deal here is conversation and companionship. Stop by and find out for yourself. From Ruthie's, the backroads journey twists through twenty-eight more miles of isolated ranches and rugged landscapes on its way to Livermore via San Antonio Valley Road. It's a trip that will take you from one urban area to another, through two friendly small communities—one high-tech and the other Old West.

Lick Observatory 408-274-5061
The Junction 408-897-3148

"The view was very extensive and the day very clear. . . . We could see various portions of the Coast Range, from far above San Francisco to below Monterey, probably 140 to 150 miles between the points, and the Diablo Range for about a hundred miles."

WILLIAM BREWER,
first known ascent of Mount Hamilton, September 1, 1861

every bend in the road reveals new views.

This backroad leads eastward from the summit to the heart of the least populated territory in the Bay Area: the San Antonio Valley, a beautifully tangled landscape of rivers and ranches reminiscent of the Old West. Life here is very different from the one most of us know. First stop—in fact, the only stop—is the Junction, a lone tavern complete with a lending library forty-five minutes down from the observatory. Locals can check out everything from the latest novel to back issues of *National Geographic* magazine; anyone can sidle up to the counter and order a cool drink or a bite to eat. If that doesn't strike your

fancy, head outside and play horseshoes.

The Junction is a kind of community center for folks who live within a thirty-mile radius. "It's a big neighborhood," explains former Junction owner Lolli Goewey, "but it's a friendly neighborhood. It's the old-time rural type of life." Many of the folks around these parts are ranchers. Some are even genuine cowboys. But to survive out here everyone has to be a little bit of everything.

Ruthie Borba knows all about community spirit. She's the owner of Ruthie's Mall, just a couple of miles down the road from the Junction. It's the kind of retail emporium that you find on the backroads. Ruthie's business is successful, even if

LOMA MAR AND PESCADERO:
Quiet Secrets of the Central Coast

Loma Mar Post Office

South of Half Moon Bay on Highway One is a beautiful site called Pescadero State Beach. It's a popular and well-known destination for many Bay Area residents as well as for visitors. But this magnificent stretch of coast has much more than beaches to offer. Just inland, in a surprisingly undisturbed pocket of the Bay Area, you can discover the towns of Pescadero and Loma Mar—communities most people race by en route to other points along the coast.

Turn inland on Pescadero Creek Road, pass the town of Pescadero (for now) and continue some eight miles to Loma Mar. You can also reach this area from Palo Alto on the same road after a winding forty-five-minute ride westward. Pescadero Creek Road is easily found off of Alpine or La Honda Roads.

As you move away from the coast you'll soon be enveloped in the quiet of a redwood forest and the little town of Loma Mar. Recently, Loma Mar was offering an impressive real estate deal: the entire town was for sale, or at least the entire downtown portion, which includes

a restaurant, a store, a volunteer fire department, one gas pump, and its own post office, complete with a postmaster. Locals here affectionately refer to themselves as Loma Martians.

Realtor Allan Bernardi is not from Loma Mar, but he knows some of the town's history. "The old families of San Francisco had their ranches in Woodside and thereabouts," says the affable realtor. "They would leave Woodside—by horse and carriage or on horseback—and come to either La Honda or to Loma Mar." These early visitors relaxed under the towering redwoods or took day rides down to the beach. Until 1941, when

Highway One was constructed, Pescadero Creek Road was one of the few routes to the coast from the growing Bay Area.

By retracing your steps on Pescadero Creek Road you can return coastward and to the town of Pescadero. During the late nineteenth century Pescadero was a booming farming, fishing, and logging town. Not only was it larger than today, but the streets were always filled with horses, carriages, and large wagons hauling logs and produce.

It might be smaller and quieter today, but the town's history and tradition are still very much alive. For example, Duarte's

Tavern has been in the same family almost continuously since the 1890s. "I figure my grandfather Cardoza came sometime in the 1870s," says Ron Duarte. His other grandfather opened the bar in 1894. Ron's children are the fourth generation to operate one of Pescadero's principal landmarks. Ron has lived in Pescadero almost all his life. "Dad built a house across the street from the restaurant in 1951. I was going to school and then I went in the service," he recalls. "I came back home in '54, stayed across the street for a couple of years, and got married in '57. Bingo! Right back up there," he laughs, pointing up to his house. "Been there ever since."

It's hard to miss Duarte's. It's right next to Pescadero's lone traffic signal. The town's business district is only one block long. It begins at Duarte's and ends at another long-standing institution—the Pescadero Community Church. This beautifully maintained church was built in 1867. Its resident minister, Orril Fluharty, hasn't been there quite that long, but he's definitely a town fixture. Although he is in his eighties, Orril can still occasionally be found shimmying giant trees as a lumberjack. "I would describe myself as a lop-eared—which I really am, one ear's a little lower than the other one—bowlegged, hard-headed, Irish lumberjack preacher," smiles Orril. "That just about sums it up for me."

But it's spiritual rather than physical challenges that Orril prefers. "The greatest pleasure," states Orril with sincerity, "the most happiness that I can get out of living, is to help someone who's down and out; to help them find a meaning for living. And the community is the same as this church. They'll get to locking horns on something and they'll go at it hammer and tong. A catastrophe comes up, something happens, and then everybody's right there to help. That's the kind of a

community it is. Of course, if I have something on my nose, and I'm up there talking in church, they'll say, 'Hey Orril! Wipe your nose!'"

While Orril is tending to Pescadero's souls, other locals—such as ecologist Toni Danzig—are helping with a different kind of renewal: restoring the vast Pescadero Marsh to its former splendor. "It's one of the last large coastal marshes on the entire West Coast," says Toni. "This is a very special place." For about a century, the marsh, sandwiched between the town and the ocean, suffered as its

fresh water was diverted for agricultural purposes. Now the water's natural flow is returning, and so is the wildlife. Bird-watching here is always good; during fall migration or during the winter you can find large flocks of ducks and shorebirds resting and feeding. In the spring the marsh comes alive with fresh greenery while marsh wrens flit about gathering nest material and raucous colonies of great blue herons raise their young in nearby eucalyptus trees.

Toni and others remember the area's human history as they preserve its natural history. The same soil and water that nurture the wildlife in the marsh—and the artichokes and other crops that are still grown nearby—have also nurtured four generations of Duartes and countless generations of coastal Indians who preceded them. "The native people must have been incredibly happy here," says Toni. "And then Europeans came, and they were happy here. Now we're here, and we're happy here. It's obviously a very healthy place. You know, in the middle of a high density population area of California, we have an anomaly, and it's called Pescadero."

Schoolchildren at Pescadero Marsh

Pescadero, Half Moon Bay Coastside
Chamber of Commerce 650-726-8380
Duarte's Tavern 650-879-0464

BIG BASIN REDWOODS STATE PARK:
Through the Forest, Looking for Things Big and Small

If you've never made the trip to Big Basin Redwoods State Park you're missing something wonderful. This landscape of soaring redwoods, cool streams, and some one hundred miles of hiking trails fills a large space in the Santa Cruz Mountains. It can take two hours to get there from San Francisco, and the final approach is on a road accented by twists and turns. But the forest is well worth the drive. Take Highway 9 to Boulder Creek (via Highways 17 or 35). Once in downtown Boulder Creek take the meandering Highway 236 for the final ten miles to the park.

Big Basin's eighteen thousand acres are dominated by ancient redwood trees. John Muir called these magnificent giants "the kings of the forest, the noblest of a noble race." Big Basin is also the place where the idea of California State Parks took root. This is the state's oldest state park, founded back in 1902 by volunteers who committed themselves to protecting endangered redwood groves throughout the Santa Cruz Mountains and elsewhere.

Their spirit still flourishes in Big Basin. Some volunteers clear and maintain trails, others will help you see what you're looking at. The volunteer trail crew is composed largely of information-age professionals who spend most of their days looking at computer screens. "They enjoy getting away from the telephone to come out and work, breathe deeply, and relax," says Bob Kirsch, the crew's leader. He continues, "when I get out here I feel like this is where I'm supposed to be. This is it!"

Mary and Sal Piazza volunteer together

COAST REDWOODS

California's coast redwood *(Sequoia sempervirens)* is the tallest—and one of the oldest—known plant species in the world. Some of these forest giants reach more than three hundred and fifty feet in Northern California; a tree felled in 1933 was 2,200 years old (most live to around six hundred years). Redwoods have played, and still play, an important role in the history, economy, and ecology of California, where the species is confined to the coastal fog belt from the Big Sur area to the Oregon border.

Waddell Creek, Big Basin Redwoods State Park

at the park's Nature Center, and they'll help you understand the park's ecology. The Piazzas are perfectly suited for the job: they have knowledge and they love to share it. Mary and Sal's lapel pins show that they have volunteered eight thousand hours, but Mary is quick to correct that number. "Actually, we have more than nine thousand hours," she says with a laugh, "but they haven't got a pin that says nine thousand." Sal adds, "These pins are out of date!"

In the midst of some of the earth's biggest trees, Sal and Mary search out the little things: Mary loves the wildflowers— which she calls "the jewels of the forest"— and Sal loves insects. When most people are hiking the trails looking up at the giant redwoods, the Piazzas teach people to stop and look down at the forest floor. If you venture out with them you might find yourself picking apart a rotting log in search of insects, or studying the intense colors of wildflowers or mushrooms. Without the insects, they explain, and all the other nutrient-recycling creatures and plants of the forest floor, the giant redwoods wouldn't survive.

These trees also couldn't have survived without a lot of help early on. Ranger Ken Morris, who has been helping people enjoy the redwoods of Big Basin since 1977, explains the importance of Slippery Rock. "This spot is famous,"

Big Basin Redwoods State Park

Big Basin Redwoods State Park

explains Ken, "because right at the base of the rock is where the Sempervirens Club met back in 1900. They were a group of concerned citizens who got together to start what is now our state park system."

Ken explains that a photographer named Andrew Hill founded the group in outrage over loggers' attempts to prevent him from taking pictures of redwoods. He and the rest of the Sempervirens Club thought these majestic trees should be accessible to everyone. After nearly a year of hard work, they prevailed and the state's first park was born.

Ken likes to think of this park as an island in the middle of a large metropolitan area. It is wild, yet accessible to millions of people. "People come here from the big city," Ken says, "and they feel like they've dropped off the edge of the earth."

The most accessible trail in Big Basin is the Redwood Trail, a short loop that takes you past some of the park's most famous trees. One of these trees is the Father of the Forest. With its huge trunk, some sixteen feet in diameter, it might look like the biggest in the park, but just keep walking. Soon you'll come to the Mother of the Forest. This tree soars 329 feet above Sal and Mary's beloved forest-floor insects and flowers. Park personnel believe it is at least a thousand years old, and possibly older. Not only that, but because most redwoods reproduce by sprouting, the Mother's root system could be tens of thousands of years old.

Another spectacular attraction of Big Basin is the waterfalls: Berry Creek Falls, Silver Falls, Golden Falls, and Cascade Falls, all accessible via the park's extensive trail system. But with a short walk visitors can easily reach Sempervirens Falls, about one and a half miles from park headquarters. It's a spectacular little waterfall, calming to the eye and the spirit.

The park's trails not only lead through miles of redwood forest (and past waterfalls), but also from ridgetops to the sea. The Skyline to Sea Trail covers eleven miles from the park headquarters down to Waddell Beach. (You can also park on Highway One and work your way gradually up to park headquarters.) As you descend, you'll find yourself alongside Waddell Creek (more like a small river, really). The creek, the valley it meanders through, and the beach are all named after William Waddell—a settler who was killed by a grizzly bear on the banks of this creek in 1875. The grizzlies are long gone, but not the stunning beauty that draws the converted and the newcomers to Big Basin every year.

Big Basin State Park 408-338-8860
State Park Volunteer Opportunities
   800-963-PARK

SAN JUAN BAUTISTA, GIZDICH RANCH, AND CAPITOLA:
The Long Way to the Coast

One of the most pleasant and easiest getaways from the Bay Area is a road trip that ends in the pretty little coastal community of Capitola. It's a journey that includes fantastic scenery, amazing produce and food, lots of California history, and sunwashed beaches.

Begin your journey to Capitola in a roundabout way. Instead of crossing over Highway 17 by Los Gatos, move south on Highway 101 until you reach the little village of San Juan Bautista in the rich agricultural lands of the San Benito Valley. It's about one hundred miles south of San Francisco, and only about forty-five miles from San Jose.

San Juan Bautista is home to a state historic park and to the largest of the California missions. It is also called home by 1,600 devoted residents. The people of this quaint town enjoy sharing their

Mission San Juan Bautista

141

village with the thousands of visitors who come to see the neatly maintained buildings of the state historic park, stroll across the old plaza, shop along the main streets, and eat in the enticing restaurants. Most notably, visitors admire the very heart and soul of San Juan Bautista: the mission.

Mission San Juan Bautista was founded on June 24, 1797, but it wasn't completed until 1812. Septuagenarian and former mayor Leonard Caetano has experienced more than one-third of San Juan Bautista's two-hundred-year history. "You know it hasn't changed very much since I was a kid," Leonard states. "And I can remember back to when I was about five years old!" But maintaining the old mission takes a lot of community effort and dedication. Over the years, the people of San Juan Bautista have worked very hard to fully restore the mission and its lovely grounds.

The mission is popular with schoolchildren from all over central California. About forty thousand kids visit the mission every year. Some days these roving packs of youngsters see little cats where big cats once roamed: if you look closely in the church you can see where mountain lions and grizzly bears left their paw prints in the adobe tiles as they dried in the untamed region that was San Juan Bautista.

The mission is more than a historic monument. It's also an active church and a center of community life. "Other than my wife and family, I think it's the most important thing," adds Leonard. It was also important to Leonard's father, Antone Caetano. In fact, Antone—who was born here in 1886—laid every brick in the mission's adobe wall.

San Juan Bautista sits on the granitic, or solid side, of the powerful San Andreas Fault. Leonard points out that if the mission had been built farther out on the alluvial side of the fault it would have been destroyed years ago. In addition to the

San Andreas Fault, the mission sits alongside another California landmark: the last original piece of the El Camino Real, once the main road that connected all twenty-one missions from San Diego to Sonoma. "It's the real McCoy," laughs Leonard. The village itself is also the real McCoy—an historic small town that gracefully caters to visitors without selling its soul.

From San Juan Bautista, head west on Highways 156 and then 129. A short passage between rolling oak-covered hills leads to open farm fields near Watsonville and the Pajaro Valley. You'll cross over the Pajaro River several times—the watery

Capitola

Mission San Juan Bautista

border between Monterey and Santa Cruz Counties. Turn off on a country road near the large Gizdich Ranch sign and you'll quickly come to a cluster of buildings. Gizdich is a family owned farm which has been a popular local institution for more than thirty years. It is also famous for its

apples and berries that you can pick yourself or purchase in the gift shop. Fresh produce, food baskets, antiques, and collectibles of all kinds line the store's shelves.

The ranch is a kid-friendly place with hay bales and tractors to play on, and

plenty of room for family picnics. Also, when you're here, you've got to have a piece of pie or take one home with you. Bakers here make Dutch apple pie, mile-high apple pie, strawberry glazed pie, and ollalaberry pie (it's kind of like blackberry, only better—it's also the *Backroads* crew's favorite!).

Properly fueled with tasty treats from Gizdich Ranch, sally forth toward the coast and find Highway One heading north to the beach town of Capitola. In about

fifteen minutes you'll reach the Capitola turnoff; about a half-mile later the ocean begins to brighten the horizon and you'll enter the center of town.

Longtime resident and bakery owner Gayle Ortiz knows Capitola's every nook

and cranny. "This town is packed with wonderful, independently owned small boutiques, dress shops, and wonderful handblown glass shops. We've got the old hippie stores across the way. You know, you don't get too many of

Soquel Creek

POINTS NORTH—SOMETHING HISTORICAL, HYSTERICAL, AND WILD

If you stay in Capitola for a few days and you want some day excursions to round out your beach schedule, consider driving northward. For a hysterical, fun-filled time motor about fifteen minutes up the coast and play at the Santa Cruz Beach and Boardwalk and Coconut Grove. Don't miss rides on the 1911 Looff carousel and the fully refurbished 1924 Big Dipper roller coaster (408-426-7433). For a dash of history hop on the Santa Cruz Big Trees and Pacific Railway train and ride to Felton. Once there, switch over to the Roaring Camp Railroad for more train time before returning to the Boardwalk via rail (408-335-4400). For a real wild time drive north on Highway One from Capitola and in about forty minutes you'll be at Año Nuevo State Reserve. This is the famous elephant seal breeding grounds (November through March; reservations recommended), but many other marine and terrestrial species can be viewed here all year (650-879-2027, recording).

---

those anymore." There is also a historic wharf (first built in the 1850s), and, not surprisingly, a gorgeous public beach.

These days Capitola is a good destination for those who love to shop and dine by the sea. The town was established in the 1860s as a resort for families— Camp Capitola—especially those trying to escape the blistering summer heat of California's interior valleys. "Capitola— and Santa Cruz County for that matter— always wanted to be for the families," says Gayle. "And we are to this day."

Families come to soak up Capitola's sun and coastal small-town charms and frolic along the waterfront just as Gayle

did when she was a little girl. Her family came from San Jose every summer. The cottage that Gayle's family once rented, and many others around town, are still available. What Gayle remembers about summers vacationing here is also true for today's children: they never take off their bathing suits, they go out to the beach first thing, and they stay there all day.

The center of town can get busy and congested during the warm months. The best thing to do is to park your car in a nearby city lot and enjoy Capitola on foot; it's only a few blocks long and very pedestrian-friendly.

If the summer crowds ever get to you

and you want a change from the beach, there are nearby places to seek refuge. One such place is a secluded creekside promenade just a stone's throw from the beach. Find the bridge crossing over Soquel Creek, face upstream, then look for the narrow path on your right (by the big interpretive sign). The path continues for about three blocks past historic buildings and old-fashioned bungalows. If you cross over to Riverview you can continue inland a few more blocks to Peery Park and a beautiful bridge. Cross over the bridge and return to the shore on Wharf Road. It's a nice walk. There is also a pleasant place to walk up on Depot Hill, a bluff-top covered with houses just south of downtown. You'll pass historic homes and some wonderful gardens.

Mission San Juan Bautista 408-623-4528
San Juan Bautista State Historic Park
    408-623-4881
San Juan Bautista Chamber of Commerce
    408-623-2454
Gizdich Ranch 408-722-1056
Rentals in Capitola,
    Vacations by the Sea Rentals
    http://www.vacation-rentals.com
Gayle's Bakery & Rosticceria
    408-462-1200
Capitola Chamber of Commerce
    408-475-6522

Central
California

From left: Debris from the filming of
The Ten Commandments, Nipomo Dunes Preserve (Tour 50),
and Monterey Bay (Tour 47)

FROM HOLLISTER TO THE CARRIZO PLAIN: Rocking and Rolling through the Heart of Central California

Virtually all of California is earthquake country. In fact, much of the state's natural beauty—soaring mountain ranges, fertile valleys, and secretive canyons—was created by seismic activity. But some places around the state are shakier than others, such as the city of Hollister, where hardly a week goes by without at least a minor tremor.

To get a good feeling for the heart of California's earthquake country, while experiencing some spectacular scenery, follow the San Andreas Fault system from Hollister's shifting sidewalks southward about a hundred miles. The route along Highways 25 and 198 and several backroads, takes you through the legendary caves and bizarre terrain of the Pinnacles National Monument. Farther on you reach the hamlet of Parkfield, where constant fault movements keep the people honest but make the bridges crooked. Then on to the Carrizo Plain—California's Serengeti—where the fault emerges like the knobby backbone of a buried dragon.

Hollister is at the junction of Highways 25 and 156, about forty miles south of San Jose. Originally a farm town and the hub of a prosperous hay-growing region, Hollister is now a booming bedroom community for San Jose. Agriculture is still important here, but most mornings find the downtown clogged with rush-hour commuters.

"We used to be called the Earthquake Capital of the World, but then the Chamber of Commerce decided that they couldn't attract new businesses with a label like that," says local merchant Bob Valenzuela. "We can't even say the word 'earthquake' in Hollister anymore. As a matter of fact, if the sheriff heard me say it, he'd put me away!"

With his trademark peace signs and his flowing white hair, Bob Valenzuela is hard to miss. Everybody in Hollister seems to know him. Bob also runs a popular video store and writes a weekly newspaper column, which he often uses to lampoon local leaders. He also likes to point out the oddities of his beloved hometown, like the town clock with its incorrect roman numeral four. "Until I brought it up," laughs Bob, "nobody even noticed it."

The San Andreas Fault runs right through Hollister, causing walls to crack and sidewalks to buckle. The western half of town is on the Pacific Plate moving toward Alaska; the other side of town sits

Bob Valenzuela

on the North American Plate and is relatively stationary. The fault movement around Hollister produces hundreds of earthquakes a year, most of which are too small to be felt. But the 1989 Loma Prieta quake caused a great deal of damage.

As you move south from Hollister on Highway 25 through the gentle landscape cradling the San Andreas fault, you'll soon come upon a unique volcanic formation straddling the fault line. This is Pinnacles National Monument, a curious landscape littered with otherworldly evidence of the earth's movements. About forty miles south of Hollister look for Highway 146 leading west to the monument (there is also a western entrance off Highway 101).

Curbside displacement from earthquake activity, Hollister

The bizarre and jumbled terrain of the monument is what remains of a volcano born in southern California 23.5 million years ago. The volcano has been carried on the back of the Pacific Plate as it scrapes its way north along the fault.

Miles of trails crisscross the Pinnacles. After moving through narrow passageways and tunnels, Ranger Peter Szydlowski points out the water in the Bear Gulch Caves. "That water you see below has carved out this narrow canyon over millions of years," he explains.

As you explore the strange geology of the monument you might find yourself standing below what may look like precariously perched boulders the size of

houses. This might seem dangerous, but it's not, according to Peter. "It's probably one of the safest places to be during an earthquake because everything has already fallen as low as it will go."

One enormous rocky cavern is called Tiburcio's Room, after a notorious bank robber who allegedly hid his loot here. The cavern is capped by one of the biggest rocks known in the state. "Legend goes," says Peter, lowering his voice, "that his ghost still haunts these caves and if anybody gets close to his hidden money, eerie green eyes shine on them and scare them off."

Among the stone formations flanking the monument's nearby reservoir is a rock

with what looks like a giant "X" carved into it. It's been nicknamed Tiburcio's X. "The bandit Tiburcio used that X as a marker to identify where his cave was," says Peter. But even if you don't find Tiburcio's booty, Pinnacles National Monument is a hidden treasure unto itself.

From Pinnacles, the San Andreas Fault—and Highway 25—slithers southward through sparsely populated ranch country en route to a mere blip on the map: the village of Parkfield, about seventy-five miles south of Pinnacles National Monument. At the junction of Highways 25 and 198 (both two-lane roads) the road becomes Highway 198; after it rises over the Parkfield Grade

(3,498 feet), it's also known as the Park-field Coalinga Road.

The Parkfield Grade begins as a nicely paved road, but the asphalt soon disappears, as do most other signs of modern civilization. When it rains, the grade is often impassable. But when the weather is clear, it's a spectacular though dusty ascent over high mountains followed by a sharp descent into a hidden valley. At the very bottom is tiny Parkfield. (You can also get to Parkfield by taking Highway 5 south to Highway 41 west or via 101 south to Highway 46 east.)

The entire town consists of one inn, one cafe, one gift shop in a caboose, a one-room schoolhouse, one extremely small library, and some high-tech equipment sequestered away in a building. When the business leaders of Hollister ran away from the title "Earthquake Capital of the World," Parkfield happily stepped in to lay claim to the name.

Duane Hamann has been carefully measuring earth movements along the fault in Parkfield for the past thirteen years. "This is the center for earthquake experiments in the world. There is more equipment in Parkfield to measure earthquake information than anyplace else," states Duane with pride and a chuckle. His task is to look for irregular-

Tiburcio's X, Pinnacles National Monument

Highway 25 near the Pinnacles

ities that might warn of a coming quake.

But Duane only moonlights as a seismic observer. By day, he is the teacher at Parkfield School, one of the few remaining one-room, kindergarten-through-sixth-grade schools in California. He's also the custodian and all-around handyman. Duane's been teaching here since 1969. In that time, he's educated two generations of Parkfield residents. "You get interested in the kids so you stay," he says.

Duane feels the same way about his work in his small seismic lab. He wants to see it through until the measurements reveal something unusual. Duane often uses a machine that sends out a laser

beam to nineteen separate reflectors positioned along the fault. By measuring how long it takes for the light to travel to and from the targets, Duane can tell how much movement there's been.

A 6.0-magnitude quake usually strikes every twenty to thirty years. At other times, the ground is creeping at a steady rate of about one-half inch per year. One of the most interesting sights in Parkfield is the town's famous bending bridge. The fault runs right down a creek and under the bridge. In the last sixty-five years, the bridge has bent about thirty inches. The earth is always shifting,

sometimes leaving destruction in its wake. Those who live along the fault have to make their peace with it.

From Parkfield your next stop is the Carrizo Plain, called California's Serengeti Plain by many. Take the Cholame Road south out of Parkfield, turn west on Highway 46 and, just past the two buildings of Cholame (home of the James Dean Memorial), turn south again on Palo Prieto-Cholame Road. The name of this road changes, and it moves through some wide open country, but it will eventually take you to Highway 58 and the "city" of California Valley on the northern edge of the Carrizo (you can also find Highway 58 off both Interstate 5 and Highway 101).

The Carrizo Plain—roughly fifty miles long and seven miles wide—is a hidden valley created by the San Andreas fault. It is one of nature's most isolated kingdoms in the country's most populated state.

Bay Area Naturalist Michael Ellis is an old friend of the Carrizo, and a frequent traveling companion of the *Backroads* crew. He often leads trips to this stark yet wildlife-packed grassland. "It might be a bit of an exaggeration to equate this place with the Serengeti, but the truth is that the Carrizo is relatively pristine and intact," he says.

One of the plain's animals is the burrowing owl, a species highly threatened elsewhere in the state. Burrowing owls are

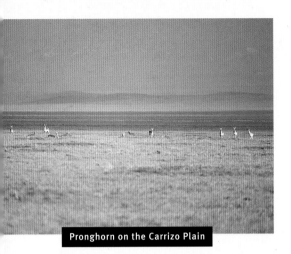

Pronghorn on the Carrizo Plain

among the only owls active in the daytime. Many of the Carrizo Plain's other denizens only come out at night. If you drive around slowly after sunset you feel as if you're on a safari: jackrabbits pop across your headlights and other night birds work the edges of the shadows. Giant kangaroo rats also live here and are one of seven species of rare and endangered animals found in the Carrizo Plain—probably the greatest concentration of endangered species anywhere in California.

The Nature Conservancy, along with the Bureau of Land Management and the California Department of Fish and Game, maintain a visitors center in the Carrizo Plain. These partners jointly manage the two hundred thousand-acre Carrizo Plain Natural Area. They strive to safeguard its vulnerable inhabitants, such as the San

Joaquin kit fox and the blunt-nosed leopard lizard, and to reintroduce once-native species like the pronghorn, elk, and bunch grasses.

Though it looks untouched, Carrizo Plain has been the site of human activity for centuries. Wheat and barley were grown here once, especially between the two world wars. But over the long haul the conditions were too dry, and ultimately the farms couldn't make it. With help, nature is reclaiming the land. Just one sign of the area's health is the amazing display of wildflowers every spring.

The plain's Painted Rock is a place where local Chumash Indians congregated for more than a thousand years, before the Spanish arrived. "Painted Rock is a place to come and nourish your soul," says Michael. "That's what the native peoples did here at Painted Rock. And, actually, that's what we come to do here today. This is a good place to come to be quiet and still and peaceful."

When you first look at the Carrizo Plain, it may appear vast and empty. But if you listen and observe you'll hear a symphony of life, particularly around Painted Rock. Snakes find shelter in the rock's crevices, ground squirrels call and scramble about, prairie falcons nest overhead, and golden eagles and ravens roost on top of the rock. Because of its sensitive wildlife and fragile pictographs, Painted

Rock is a specially protected area—you can only visit as part of a regularly scheduled tour.

"The Carrizo," explains Michael, "is one of those places, that, if you weren't looking carefully and just drove through, you'd say, 'What's the big deal?' It's not easy to understand the beauty and the diversity of this place. But if you look closely you can see how everything is connected."

The San Andreas fault runs right along the Temblor Mountain Range—the eastern border of the plain. It's perhaps one of the best places in the world to see fault activity on the earth's surface. "This place was a power spot to native Californians," says Michael. "They believed that when you came into this valley, it shook if you made the spirits angry. That was an excellent interpretation of the San Andreas Fault because it does shake here. It shakes a lot."

Hollister B.O.B.'s Video 408-637-0737
Pinnacles National Monument
    408-389-4485
The Parkfield Inn and Cafe 805-463-2421
Carrizo Plain Visitor Center 805-475-2131
Michael Ellis's Footloose Forays
    707-829-1844
California Valley Ranch & Resort
    805-475-2363

MONTEREY:
History, Charm, Fish, and Fun

Monterey has long been known as a tourist destination, and rightly so. Fisherman's Wharf, Cannery Row, and the Monterey Bay Aquarium attract hundreds of thousands of visitors each year. After all, for natural beauty, friendly people, and wonderful food, it's one of the state's great treasures. And best of all, it's just down the road.

But the Monterey area is more than a haven for tourists, it's also a real community, much of which you can easily explore by foot. Hardly more than a hundred miles south of San Francisco, and only about an hour from San Jose, the city of Monterey shares a lovely peninsula with the towns of Carmel and Pacific Grove. Carmel Valley is nearby and Big Sur is a short drive south along Highway One.

John Pisto has lived his entire life in Monterey. He owns four restaurants, he has written books and hosts a television show on Monterey cooking, and he enjoys taking a one-mile walk through town. He starts on the old commercial wharf early in the morning. "I tell you," says John chuckling, "when the sun is coming up, and you're walking down here, you never know what you're going to see."

Monterey pelicans

Against a backdrop of fishing boats, bickering gulls, and barking sea lions, John marvels that more people don't explore the old commercial wharf and discover its sights and sounds. It's a working harbor where you can see fisherman haul in their catches at dawn.

From the commercial wharf John wanders inland to view the many faces of Monterey's old town around the Stanton Center (a museum and visitor center). Many buildings in Monterey's old section are now part of a state historic park. Throughout, he finds quiet, hidden gardens, benches for resting, and a distinct feeling of a time long ago.

John likes to stop at the town's old whaling station, situated on Decatur Street.

It has barely changed since it was used by Portuguese whalers in the 1850s. If you look closely at the paving stones around the building, you'll see that some are actually sections of gray whale vertebrae.

Next to the whaling station is the state's first brick building. Both the brick building and the station were erected in 1847. Nearby, many other structures remain from that time, when this was a small but bustling town and California's first capital.

The early nineteenth century Customs House was another important landmark in old Monterey, and it's nearby, too. Ships unloaded their cargo here to be inspected and taxed by government officials. Today it houses exhibits that describe the era and the goods that passed through these

doors long ago. The state historic park has an excellent map to help you wind your way through this area; pick one up at the Stanton Center.

"I'd like people to understand that Monterey is a small community," says John. "What we're doing is what people should be doing when they come down here. Get out of the car and walk around. Enjoy these beautiful gardens, enjoy the buildings."

There are fish markets where you'll find everything from bocaccio (with their gaping mouths) to prized salmon and delicious Pacific grenadier, also known by the unappetizing name of rattail. When you're near Fisherman's Wharf, the best thing to do is eat. You name it in the fresh-seafood category—fish, shrimp, squid, oysters, crab—and you'll be able to find it here.

Monterey and its surrounds beckon walkers and runners, and much of the area is accessible to people who use wheelchairs. One example is the fabulous Monterey Bay Coastal Trail—an easy path following the rugged water's edge for miles. The best-developed portion of the trail stretches all the way from Monterey to Pacific Grove. This portion is also home to the 1855 Point Pinos Light Station, one of the oldest continuously operating light-houses on the West Coast.

On the Carmel side of the peninsula

it's possible to walk through natural areas that remain largely undeveloped, especially at the southern edge of town near the mouth of the Carmel Valley. There, at the Carmel River State Beach, where the Carmel River flows into the sea during wet winters, you'll discover a spectacular white sandy beach and several miles of easy trails to explore.

If you want get in your car and drive a little, there's even more to see. Start along the coast in Pacific Grove. Then, pay the reasonable toll to take the famous Seventeen-Mile Drive and marvel at the beauty of the shoreline. A little inland, you can visit the 525-acre Jacks Peak County Park (off of Highway 68). The road through the park climbs to reveal marvelous vistas. Through impressive stands of Monterey pines you can see to the north and west and take in the Monterey Peninsula and the deep blue waters of the Pacific. Southward is Carmel Valley and the Santa Lucia Mountains that form the backdrop of Big Sur. Taking in the view from Jacks Peak is an excellent way to top off your visit, because you'll soon realize there is a lot more to come back for.

Monterey State Historic Park
408-649-7118
Monterey Peninsula Visitors and Conference Bureau 408-649-1770

POINT LOBOS AND BIG SUR:
The Face of the Earth, As It Was Intended to Look

48

Many people believe that there is no place more beautiful than California's central coast, especially the region from Monterey and Carmel south through Big Sur along historic Highway One. Without a doubt, for sheer wild beauty and open spaces, the legendary Big Sur coast is hard to beat.

Big Sur is a ninety-mile stretch of coast extending from approximately Carmel down to Hearst Castle in San Simeon, and inland to the Santa Lucia Mountains within the Los Padres National Forest. All through this magnificent landscape travels Highway One—a ribbon of concrete hugging the very edge of the continent.

Everybody has his or her own idea of exactly where Big Sur begins. But most locals would probably say that Big Sur starts just south of Carmel at San Jose Creek State Beach, more commonly

A beach at Julia Pfeiffer Burns State Park

Point Lobos State Reserve

known as Monastery Beach. Southward from this shoreline the land grows wild. The wildness is especially visible and accessible at one of the best places to start a visit to the northern portion of Big Sur: Point Lobos State Reserve. This crown jewel of the region juts out into the aquamarine waters of the Pacific immediately south of Monastery Beach.

The reserve was formed in 1933 when a few hundred acres were purchased to help save the area's Monterey cypress. Today the reserve takes in more than 1,300 acres, many of which are underwater—a scuba diver's paradise. The reserve's biological richness becomes apparent when you realize that more than two hundred and fifty wildlife species and more than three hundred and fifty plant species have been recorded here.

One of this area's most famous residents, Clint Eastwood, is a passionate admirer of Point Lobos. Clint has made Carmel his home since 1951, and he won Carmel's mayoral election in 1984. "Once you spend some time in this country, it gets in your blood, and the place just sticks with you," says Clint. "It's infectious."

Clint suggests that the best way to enjoy Point Lobos is by foot. Just pick any trail and it will lead you to some of nature's most dazzling sights: sunning harbor seals, nesting cormorants, frolicking sea otters, and much more. "You can come out to Point Lobos on slow days and have it all to yourself," says Clint. "In the summer a lot of people come here but it never gets crowded." The reserve avoids overcrowding thanks to its policy of regulating the number of visitors at peak times (during midsummer weekends you might have to wait a bit to get in, but it's worth it).

Clint adds, "With my busy life, a place like this is crucial. It allows me to relax. It's also a great place for families. I just feel really lucky to be part of it."

Following Highway One south of Point Lobos—as the road struggles to fit the contours of the demanding terrain—the dramatic scenery and rugged coastline

Bixby Bridge

> "Noon found us at Point Lobos. It is a superb headland overgrown with pines and cypresses that lean in perilous balance over the crashing sea, or stand statuesquely on rocky ledges, ideally pictorial."
>
> J. SMEATON CHASE,
> *California Coast Trails— A Horseback Ride from Mexico to Oregon, 1913*

soon reveal themselves. Big Sur is a landscape that compels many of us to visit, but it repels most of us from living here. In many respects it's overwhelming: one minute it's calm and warm, and the next it's windy and fog-covered. As one local resident put it, "Either it takes you in, or it says, 'I'm sorry, you can't stay.'" Because Big Sur is both beautiful and challenging, families living here must be self-sufficient; they often must deal with natural disasters such as flooding, landslides, and frequent road closures.

Tomi Lussier is a longtime resident and the author of *Big Sur: A Complete History and Guide*. She explains that Highway One was begun in the 1920s and finally completed in 1937. "In many ways the road is Big Sur. It's the amphitheater

to Big Sur because without the road we couldn't look at the views." In addition to the road itself, there are some twenty-nine bridges along the way, some quite well-known such as the 1932 Bixby Bridge.

Although Tomi lost her sight in an accident in the early 1980s, she continues her writing with the help of a special computer. She also clearly recalls the beauty of her home. "Big Sur is different around each corner of the road, depending on the weather—the clouds or the way the fog is sitting on the hillsides. There might be wildflowers in a meadow that weren't there the day before, or the colors of the mountains could be different—they are brown and dry in the summer and emerald green in the winter. Everything is always changing."

Highway One acts as something of a freedom trail for city-weary folks who long to be in a place that is still mostly unpaved. In addition to interesting little communities—and some self-proclaimed characters and eccentrics—Big Sur is also home to thousands of acres of parkland. Just south of Point Sur and its historic light station (a great place to tour on weekends during nonwinter months), Highway One approaches the Big Sur Valley, an area once famous for Monterey Jack cheese. This area was Andrew Molera's ranch, and developers would love to get their hands on its rare flat land and gentle rising

ridge. Fortunately for us, it's now a large state park that bears Molera's name.

The Big Sur River—a beautiful waterway only ankle-deep in summer but deep and powerful after winter storms—runs right through the park. Whether you're camping in the park's meadow, marveling at driftwood sculptures on the long beach, hiking ridgelines above the sea, or spotting whales on their seasonal migration, Molera is a special place. There are no houses here and no congestion, just you and Big Sur. State Park Ranger Ken Lee knows the peace and serenity of the region very well. "Things quiet down at night and you find yourself going to bed during the winter at eight or nine o'clock in the evening. Maybe even on a Friday night!"

Just south of Andrew Molera is Pfeiffer Big Sur State Park and another of the region's special places: Sycamore Canyon. Just follow the well-marked sign and turn west off Highway One toward the Pacific, slow down for the quail, cross Pfeiffer Creek, and about two miles later you'll discover Pfeiffer Beach.

The lands of Big Sur are riddled with human history, and some historic buildings—such as Molera's Pioneer Cabin—are open to visitors. But something new to the area is the return of a species that once soared above the Santa Lucia Mountains and scavenged along the shore before humans arrived on the scene: California condors.

Condors, once near extinction, are trying to fit into the Big Sur landscape again with the help of dedicated biologists and the Ventana Wilderness Sanctuary. "We are putting some of the pieces of the ecological puzzle back in that have fallen out," says Susan Sachs of the sanctuary staff. "You hear so much doom and gloom today that it's just nice to say 'Hey we think we have a success story.' We don't know if the reintroduction of condors is going to work yet, but we hope so."

Author Henry Miller once wrote that Big Sur was "the face of the earth as it was intended to look." How true. There is no question that Big Sur is remote, and if you stay in one of its high-end resorts, it can be expensive. But the most important things here—the real reasons for coming down to Big Sur—are absolutely free.

Point Lobos State Reserve (and Garrapata State Park) 408-624-4909
Big Sur Chamber of Commerce 408-667-2100
Point Sur State Historic Park 408-625-4419
Andrew Molera State Park & Pfeiffer Big Sur State Park 408-667-2315
Condor Information, Ventana Wildlife Sanctuary 408-624-1202

FORESTIERE:
Fresno's Amazing Underground Gardens

The backroads always lead to unforgettable experiences and characters, even in the most unlikely of places. Take Fresno, for example, about halfway between Modesto and Bakersfield in the San Joaquin Valley. Right next to a busy Fresno street crammed with fast-food restaurants is an underground oasis—an intricate network of passageways, living quarters, trees growing through skylights, and beautiful courtyards. It's called the Forestiere Underground Gardens. "Or, if you're Sicilian," says Mark Forestiere, "the *Forestieri* Underground Gardens." Mark should know; he is the grand-nephew of Baldisare Forestiere—the man who built the gardens and lived here from 1906 to 1946.

Mark and his family have devoted themselves to restoring and protecting Baldisare's unique legacy, stretched out across five acres of land that the family could easily sell for a great deal of money. "It's a thing of great joy to us," Mark explains. "Just like the poet said, 'a thing of beauty is a joy forever.' There is so much beauty here." A visit to the gardens

Underground bedroom at Forestiere Underground Gardens

Forestiere Underground Gardens

grow above ground because their roots hit the hardpan, I'll plant them under the ground one by one by one.'" One result of this ingenious design is that you can walk above ground and collect fruit at eye level! But Baldisare actually started building his underground castle to escape the area's brutal summer heat. While temperatures can easily exceed a hundred and ten degrees above ground, they're usually in the seventies down below.

Forestiere Underground Gardens is located in Fresno just off Highway 99 at 5021 West Shaw Avenue, about a four-hour drive southeast from the Bay Area. Fresno is known mostly as a commercial hub of the San Joaquin Valley, but in the spring, the area's orchards explode into the spectacular sixty-seven-mile blossom trail, and the rolling hills on the eastern outskirts of town lead to the delights of Yosemite and Sequoia National Parks.

Altogether, Baldisare's underground orchard numbers about a hundred fruit trees of many kinds, and they are a true joy to behold. The next time you are passing through Fresno between early June and Labor Day, stop in at the gardens to cool off, and marvel at the genius of Baldisare Forestiere.

is more than just a tour of a surprising and mysterious place. You'll take away a sense of awe that one man—by himself and in his spare time—could have built this subterranean kingdom, and that his family has sacrificed so much to preserve it.

"Before Baldisare died in 1946, my grandfather would visit him in the hospital. Baldisare would say, 'If anything happens to me, take care of my gardens,'" recalls Mark. "And before my grandfather passed away, he asked my dad the same thing. And I'm sure Dad will ask the same thing of

us." Instead of relaxing during his retirement years, Mark's dad is hard at work following his father's wishes. And he's also doing it for people he doesn't even know—visitors from around the world whom Mark's father calls "aesthetic pilgrims."

The ground where Baldisare decided to construct his masterpiece is extremely hard-packed earth. So, he had to crack through it with picks and shovels. Besides having a strong back, Baldisare had a creative mind that helped him reap the fruit of his labors. According to Mark, "He thought, 'Well, if I can't get my trees to

Forestiere Underground Gardens

209-271-0734

50

SAN LUIS OBISPO: Northern California's Southernmost Town

San Luis Obispo is almost exactly halfway between San Francisco and Los Angeles. Some people think of this thriving coast-side community as the gateway to southern California. But it can also be viewed as the southernmost city in northern California.

San Luis Obispo is a spirited city of about forty-three thousand people gathered around the hills of the Santa Lucia Range off of Highway 101 about 230 miles south of San Francisco. It's a place where history is alive and well.

The town got its start in 1772, when Father Junípero Serra established Mission San Luis Obispo de Tolosa. The town grew up around the mission. San Luis Obispo seems to honor its history more than most West Coast cities. Bill Cattaneo, a

Mission San Luis Obispo de Tolosa

local historian and one of the town's biggest boosters, points out that Muzio's, an Italian grocery store, was founded in 1888 and has only had three owners. "When my grandmother first came here from Italy in 1913," recalls Bill, "this is where she did her first shopping."

San Luis is fun to explore on foot. Virtually everything feels within reach. And every Thursday night downtown bustles with another tradition—a lively farmers market. Thousands of people show up each week to buy fresh produce and other goods and to socialize.

As the midpoint for those traveling between the Bay Area and southern California, San Luis has long offered many clean, moderately priced motels. In fact, for more than seventy years this has been one of America's motel meccas. And for those travelers who keep track of such things, San Luis is home to the world's first motel. It's called the Motel Inn, and it was built back in 1925 when a couple dozen cars might pass through town daily.

Bob Davis owns the Motel Inn. It's closed now, but someday he hopes to turn it into a museum. "Some of us have memories of those drives before the interstates," says Bob, "when there was a lot more interest and texture to travel. Not everything was a franchise. In fact, *nothing* was a franchise."

The Motel Inn may be San Luis's

Debris from the filming of *The Ten Commandments*, Nipomo Dunes Preserve

oldest motel, but not most famous. That distinction belongs to the Madonna Inn, just outside of town, where every room has a theme. You can sleep in the Cave Man Room, or you can try the Love Nest. But a perennial favorite here is free of charge, and it's always worth a stop: the outrageously designed bathrooms!

A short drive south of San Luis Obispo puts you on the beach—literally—and still on the trail of history. At the Oceano Dunes State Vehicular Recreation Area there was once an isolated and most unusual community. Beginning in the early 1900s, these dunes sheltered a small group of intellectuals and free spir-

its who sought peace and solitude. They were painters, writers, and poets, and they came to be known as the Dunites. Local author Norm Hammond knows their history well. "I think they were searching for the same thing that I'm searching for, and that all of us are, really," states Norm, "a better way to live. They wanted to be more free. They wanted to know one's place in the universe."

The last of the Dunites left in 1974. All that remains is a cabin that belonged to Gavin Arthur, grandson of president Chester A. Arthur and the leader of the Dunites in the 1930s. The cabin was later moved to the nearby town of Oceano, and stands as a fragile reminder of the Dunites' dream for a better life.

If you drive farther south, through the town of Guadalupe and into the Nature Conservancy's Nipomo Dunes Preserve, you'll find more dunes and a buried treasure: the original set for the 1923 film extravaganza *The Ten Commandments*. Cecil B. DeMille's blockbuster featured a cast of thousands and perhaps the largest movie set ever built. After the filming was completed, the set was knocked over and left in the dunes. Over time wind and rain and shifting sand have reduced DeMille's monument to thousands of little pieces of wood and plaster and rusty nails.

From fragments of Hollywood's glory, to the nearly forgotten dreams of a better world in the dunes, to a vision of pleasant dreams for tired motorists in the world's first motel, the past blends easily with the present along the scenic southern edge of northern California.

San Luis Obispo County Visitors and
    Conference Bureau 800-634-1414
Madonna Inn 805-543-3000
Oceano Dunes State Vehicular Recreation
    Area 805-473-7223
Nature Conservancy's Guadalupe-Nipomo
    Dunes Preserve 805-546-8378

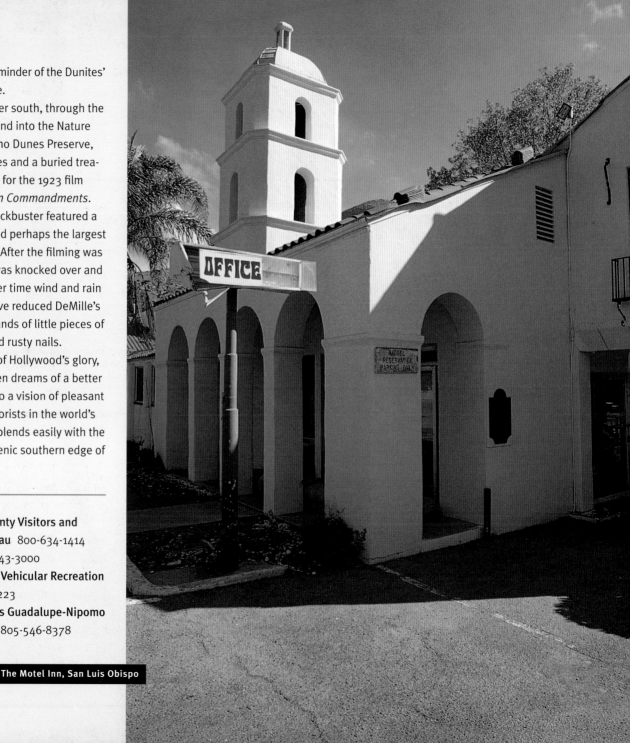

The Motel Inn, San Luis Obispo

Index